Forests Adrift

Forests Adrift

*Currents Shaping the Future of
Northeastern Trees*

CHARLES D. CANHAM

Yale UNIVERSITY PRESS

New Haven and London

Published with assistance from the Louis Stern Memorial Fund.

Yale University Press books may be purchased in quantity for educational, business, or promotional use. For information, please e-mail sales.press@yale.edu (U.S. office) or sales@yaleup.co.uk (U.K. office).

Set in Minion type by IDS Infotech, Ltd.
Printed in the United States of America.

Library of Congress Control Number: 2019945868
ISBN 978-0-300-23829-7 (hardcover : alk. paper)

A catalogue record for this book is available from the British Library.

This paper meets the requirements of ANSI/NISO Z39.48-1992 (Permanence of Paper).

10 9 8 7 6 5 4 3 2 1

To Judy, for indulging my walks in the woods

Contents

Acknowledgments

The material in this book grows out of over forty years spent studying forests, and even longer being fascinated by trees. I was lucky to have a wildly different set of mentors to get me started in science. Theodore (Tad) Weaver at Montana State University, Orie Loucks at the University of Wisconsin, and Peter Marks at Cornell University were incredibly generous with their time and wisdom and very personal approaches to science. I don't think I could ever match Tad's boundless energy, Orie's passion for science in the public interest, or the craftsmanship of Peter's work, but each of them inspired me. I owe an even greater debt of gratitude to Gene Likens, my postdoctoral adviser and the founder of the Institute of Ecosystem Studies, for giving me the intellectual freedom to pursue such a wide range of research and, through the institute and my colleagues there, the perfect setting in which to do it. Joshua Ginsberg, the current president of the Cary Institute of Ecosystem Studies, has my thanks not just for encouraging me to focus my efforts on reaching new audiences, but even more for the sense of energy and excitement he has brought to guiding the future of the Institute.

I have been fortunate to work with a wonderful group of graduate students and postdocs over the years, and with many

collaborators in the United States and abroad. Their friendship
and our many experiences in the field (and countless but good-
natured meetings) have meant a great deal to me. I'd particularly like to thank my colleagues K. David Coates in British
Columbia and Christian Messier in Quebec for sharing my
commitment to melding fieldwork to models. I'd also like to
thank my colleagues John Pastor, Peter Marks, Joshua Ginsberg,
and Gary Lovett for their comments on the manuscript. Leo
Destremps, master carpenter and boatbuilder in Newport,
Rhode Island, introduced me over forty years ago to the importance of sharp tools in any craft. Twenty-five years ago
Stephen Pacala introduced me to a new set of scientific tools,
one based on likelihood statistical methods and models, which
transformed my craft as a scientist.

I have had the opportunity to study forests in many parts
of the world, but none have been as dear to me as my long-term
study sites at Great Mountain Forest in Norfolk, Connecticut.
For almost one hundred years the stewardship and progressive
forest management of Great Mountain by the Childs family and
staff have created an ideal site for ecological research. I'd like to
thank the family and particularly Jody Bronson, the longtime
forester at Great Mountain, for supporting my work there.
Through the generosity of the Childs family Great Mountain is
now protected in perpetuity in the nonprofit Great Mountain
Forest Corporation.

As much as I love walking through the history-laden oak
forests of southern New England, the vast and almost primeval
forests of the Adirondacks of New York are just as important
to me. It has been a privilege to serve on the boards of the Adirondack Chapter of The Nature Conservancy, the Adirondack
Land Trust, the Adirondack Council, and the Northern Forest
Atlas Foundation. My thinking about the future of those forests

has been shaped by countless discussions with staff and board members from those and the other nonprofits that have been so passionate about protecting that marvelous landscape. I would particularly like to thank Ed McNeil, the former board chair of the Adirondack Chapter of The Nature Conservancy, for his friendship and for constantly prodding me to step out from my academic shell. Three summers and several hundred hours in the back seat of his AirCam, while he piloted us to sample hundreds of lakes in the Adirondacks, gave me an unprecedented view several hundred feet above millions of acres of forest canopy. It was also through my work in the Adirondacks that I met Jerry Jenkins. Jerry's photography, illustrations, and writing elevate natural history to an art form. Our talks and walks always inspire and inform me.

As important as my field research has been to me, for most of the past decade I have worked almost exclusively with the remarkable scientific resource provided by the Forest Inventory and Analysis program of the U.S. Forest Service. The rigorous statistical design of this nationwide network of forest inventory plots, combined with meticulous sampling by the field crews and the speed with which their data are made available to researchers, are all really quite extraordinary.

Science has always been a very personal endeavor for me, but very little of it would have been possible without public funding from American, Canadian, and New Zealand government agencies. In the United States I would particularly like to thank the National Science Foundation for the many different grants that have supported my work over the past thirty years.

I suspect that I could have easily spun out my research career happily writing more peer-reviewed scientific papers. I was fortunate that Jean Thomson Black of Yale University Press was in the audience for a talk I gave at a natural history conference several years ago. It was a rare event where the organizers gave me ninety minutes to speak—a very dangerous thing with me because it meant I could try to weave together the many threads I'd been working on over the years. Jean tracked me down afterward and encouraged me to try my hand at writing up that material for a broader audience. Her support and advice throughout have been invaluable.

Each fall for the past thirty-four years I have led a short hike for the public along one of the nature trails at the Cary Institute. It would be interesting to reconstruct how the natural history stories I tell have changed over that time. The vegetation has certainly changed and new threats have emerged. I'd like to thank the folks who've come along on those walks for their questions and their interest and for giving me the chance to hone my storytelling. And I have always thought of even very technical science writing as storytelling—just with lots of rules about what you can include and how you tell it. But ultimately the story has to hold together.

It was on one of those walks that I met Amy Goldman Fowler, a neighbor, noted author, and someone I learned shared my interests in the ecological history of the fields and forests of the Hudson Valley. Her encouragement and friendship and the support of the Lillian Goldman Charitable Trust convinced me to finally commit to this project. I am extraordinarily grateful to her.

Forests Adrift

Introduction

Forests Adrift captures my thoughts on the future of the forests of the northeastern United States, one of the country's most thoroughly forested regions. A central theme of this story is that the notion of a primeval condition still has a great hold on both our emotions and understanding of these forests. For my earliest research I worked in what was at that time the largest known old-growth forest remaining in the northeastern United States: a roughly fifty-thousand-acre tract in the Adirondack Mountains of New York. And while it was clear to me that those uncut remnants of the original forests were rare, they were thought to serve as an important baseline for our understanding of what the landscape was and could become. Looking back, I see that the human footprint was and is everywhere. There could still be value in studying forests in pristine conditions—if such a thing could actually be found—but only to serve as a depressing baseline against which to measure the threats that human activities pose.

Our preoccupation with the idea of a primeval forest is reinforced by a body of ecological theory and research embedded in notions that these forests can be understood in a framework of disturbance and recovery. There is a comforting assumption of stability and steady state implicit in the notion of recovery. Ecologists have been questioning this assumption for decades. And the silos of research that have grown up to understand the many ways in which human activities threaten our forests have struggled to place their work in any formal theory of forest dynamics, particularly one as simple as disturbance followed by recovery to steady state. I have spent some time in most of those silos and have finally come to at least a conceptual model of how I think about forest futures under all of the various currents that will shape those futures. The framework is avowedly empirical and based on demography: the study of the birth, growth, and death of the individual trees that make up a forest. It largely abandons the comfort of an ideal of even hypothetical return to primeval conditions in favor of accepting that forests drift. Like the forests, I'm learning to go with the flow and try to understand where the forests are currently headed.

Over the past fifty years we ecologists have explored ever more quantitative and abstract models of forest dynamics. We started to ponder "domains of attraction" and "multiple stable states" and began to search for workable definitions of resilience as a measure of the strength of the return to a steady state following disturbance. The emergence of notions of chaos and developments in complex systems theory offered a different way of thinking about forest dynamics—one that was far less predictable. There might still be a steady state lurking somewhere, but the destination was of much less interest than the twists and turns that forests take along the way.

While I appreciate the elegant simplicity that abstract models can possess, none of them is capable of encompassing the full range of currents that our forests face today. Instead, I have fallen back on the simple empiricism of a demographer.

Ultimately, changes in the distribution and abundance of tree species can be broken down and analyzed in terms of the simple vital rates of birth, growth, and death. There isn't much theoretical elegance in demographic models, but they have the benefit of being almost infinitely flexible. For over twenty-five years I have been working with a simple demographic model of forest dynamics informed by as much field data as I can assemble. If I squint I can see general and almost equilibrial patterns implied by the data and the model, but a more clear-eyed look reveals an almost infinite variety of possible futures. The current trajectory of a stand of trees might, in fact, have a stable endpoint at some time in the distant future. But given how frequently our forests are buffeted by diverse and increasingly unpredictable forces, stability is of academic interest only.

Forests Adrift surveys the human impacts I believe will have the greatest influence on the future of northeastern US forests. My goal is not to review the large bodies of research on those threats but rather to put them in the context of their potential future impact on changes in the distribution and abundance of tree species. This endeavor will include legacies of human activities dating as far back as European settlement, which transformed the landscape with consequences that could well last for centuries more to come. Fire suppression over the past century has already ushered in forests with compositions that have no analog in the twelve thousand years since the retreat of the glaciers. Climate change almost certainly is an existential threat to these forests, but my research suggests that its influence on the distribution and abundance of our native tree species will pale in comparison to the effects of many other human activities, at least for the next two hundred to four hundred years. Logging currently accounts for roughly 60 percent of annual tree mortality in eastern forests, and logging regimes can change rapidly in response to a wide range of social and economic pressures. Ecologists routinely ignore logging in their thinking about the regional distribution and abundance of tree species, and yet current selective logging practices strongly favor more shade-tolerant species. Historically high deer populations have pervasive impacts on tree regeneration throughout northeastern forests and are almost certainly depressing regional forest productivity by as much as 25 percent. On the other hand, air pollution in the form of nitrogen deposition is fertilizing these forests and could be increasing regional productivity by 40 percent. The effects of nitrogen deposition are highly selective, however. While some species benefit from the added nitrogen, others, particularly ones adapted to soils that are naturally low in nitrogen, suffer higher mortality. And the long-term effects of saturating forest soils with all that nitrogen remain a serious concern.

Many forest ecologists would rank the introduction of new forest pests and pathogens as the most serious threat facing eastern US forests. What could be more profound than the virtual elimination of the American chestnuts and elms and butternuts, the diminution of American beech, and the ongoing decimation of hemlocks and all of our ash species? And there is little reason to believe that that litany is complete. If anything, the rate of introduction of new pests and pathogens is accelerating. Although species are effectively lost—but not extinct, at least not yet, although butternut may claim that dubious distinction—forests remain. But the decimation of native tree species represents a fundamental change in our forest futures.

There is a doomsayer thread in much of the public attention paid to these threats. It would be easy to blame university press offices and reporters looking for catchy headlines. In 1986 the *New York Times* carried an article with the headline "Sugar

Maple Faces Extinction Threat." According to "forestry experts,"
the prediction "follows a rapid decline in the tree population
caused . . . by acid rain and other pollution." It turns out that
the decline in question was almost entirely limited to damage
to leaves within tree crowns rather than declines in the actual
abundance of sugar maple. Sugar maple is more abundant now
than it was in 1986 and probably more abundant than at any
time in the past four hundred years, given its rise in abundance
in oak forests as a result of fire suppression. But researchers
bear some of the blame. There is a natural tendency to begin
new research by saying, "I study this because it is important."
But it is also human nature that after you have devoted years
of research to a subject, the perspective can morph into "This
is important because I study it." And the easiest way to get
attention for your research is to highlight dangers you have
uncovered. Given the social, political, and economic forces
arrayed against addressing the myriad threats our forests face,
it is understandable that most attention is focused on dire
predictions.

As a generalist I have been primarily interested in how
these myriad forces alter the underlying distribution and abundance of our tree species. My research has made me if not
iconoclastic at least guardedly optimistic about the future of our
forests. While our forests may be adrift, I still have a lot of faith
that they will remain afloat. It is hard to strike a balance between
Pollyanna and Chicken Little, and my own emotions tend to
oscillate between the two extremes. The current pace of change
in the forces that shape the distribution and abundance of tree
species is clearly unprecedented, whether it is due to climate
change, the introduction of new pests and pathogens, changes
in forestry practices, or the interactions of these and other drivers of change. And yet our native tree species have been shaped

over millions of years of evolution for their tolerance of highly variable and often stressful environmental conditions. There is neither compelling theory nor robust empirical evidence to lead us to believe that our forests are resilient in the technical way ecologists use that term—namely, that our forests have stabilizing mechanisms that steer them back to some nominal steady state—except in the most basic sense that they remain forests consisting of a closed canopy of at least one species of tree. Rather, there is every reason to believe that our forests will continue to drift and even at times be buffeted in response to so many disparate forces. And any change in the composition of tree species in a stand has cascading control over the rich array of ecosystem services that a forest provides. It seems inescapable that our forests will be poorer in native species, at least until we figure out how to fight back against the spread of new pests and pathogens. We should also expect that there will be unprecedented assemblages of both native and introduced species in our forests. This has been touted as a hallmark of the new Anthropocene, but it is clear that the emergence of novel ecosystems has been in the works for centuries.

I hope that *Forests Adrift* will provide anyone interested in the future of our forests with a sense of the currents at work but also with a sense of the limitations in our ability to truly forecast change more than a few decades into the future. This is not a failure or inadequacy of our science. I have come to believe that it is a fundamental aspect of the nature of our forests. Even after forty years of working to understand the ecology of eastern forests, including twenty-five years combining intensive field research with a state-of-the-art computer model, I have little faith in our ability to predict where this ship will end up. All we can do at this point is say where it is currently headed.

1

Where Is the Crew, and Just What Ship Are We On, Anyway?

Its title notwithstanding, this book is about trees. More specifically, it is a book about the trees growing in upland forests of the northeastern United States. And although swamps share many species with the uplands, the issues in wetlands are too different to encompass here. The saying "can't see the forest for the trees" implies failure to see the big picture while being overwhelmed with minor detail. But in the ways that matter most to me as an ecologist, the forest *is* the trees. Trees comprise the bulk of the living and dead biomass in a forest, and they structure the environment and habitat for all of the other organisms that live there. And each species of tree has a unique ecological footprint that overlaps and interacts with the influence of their immediate neighbors to create an almost infinite variety of conditions within a forest.

Scientists appear to have a compelling need to lump this variability into a manageable number of forest types that can be named. There is even an official national standard for classifying all of the vegetation of the country into a nested series of more and more finely divided categories.[1] It has taken over twenty years to get even a fraction of the dozens of federal, state, and nongovernmental organizations that manage natural resources to adopt those standards. While I understand the practical benefits of grouping and classifying forests, the intellectual merits of that effort have been debated for over a century. It is fair to say that the "classifiers" have won the day on practicality, but well-established ecological principles require that they acknowledge that the categories are artificial constructs.

This is all by way of saying that I have never encountered a set of names or grouping of northeastern forest types that I liked or found very useful. And my academic lineage predisposes me to question the intellectual foundation of any classification system. One hundred years ago Frederick Clements was one of the most influential figures in the young field of plant ecology. He proposed that groups of species consistently co-occurred in discrete associations and at least implicitly equated them to different organisms. But within just a few years Clements's ideas were questioned by Henry Gleason, whose studies led him to believe that species were distributed individualistically along environmental gradients. Gleason's ideas came to be known as the individualistic hypothesis. Clements's perspective held sway for decades, and Gleason abandoned ecology and became one of the country's most prominent plant taxonomists, spending much of his career at the New York Botanical Garden. But by the 1950s John Curtis at the University of Wisconsin and Robert Whittaker (eventually of Cornell University) were championing Gleason's hypothesis and emphasizing that, while species certainly interacted, their unique natural histories led to overlapping but separate distributions of those species along environmental gradients.[2]

I did graduate work at both Wisconsin and Cornell, where I was steeped in the work of Curtis and Whittaker and thus have to admit some potential bias in favor of Gleason's hypothesis. But in the forty years I have been active in ecology I have seen no serious empirical or intellectual challenge to their ideas. At this point I think it is entirely appropriate to elevate Gleason's hypothesis to the status of a principle of ecology.

So when I walk in the woods I expect to find and indeed do find a vast diversity of mixtures of tree species present. In fact, if you collect a set of samples from forest plots distributed randomly and therefore representatively across the landscape, you will find almost all possible combinations of mixtures of tree species, given the environmental limits of each species. If Clements had been right, we should see distinct clustering of plots into different associations.[3]

The evidence that tree species are sorted individualistically along a variety of environmental gradients is overwhelming. For the Northeast as a whole the most obvious gradient is the variation in climate from north to south. The region contains a number of species, particularly some of our most abundant conifers, including northern white cedar, balsam fir, and red spruce, that are at or near the southern limits of their ranges across northern New York and New England (fig. 1). We also have many species, particularly most of our oak species, that are at or near their northern range limits in southern New England (fig. 2). As a result, the most basic division of the region is between northern and southern forests. Most forest ecologists would consider these distinctly different ecosystems, even if there is no consensus on exactly what to call them. In between is an area of transition (covering much of Massachusetts) with elements of both forests. Figures 1 and 2 show only a small portion of the geographic ranges of the eighteen most common species in northeastern forests, and there are many tree species that are common throughout the region, regardless of climate. In fact, the five most abundant

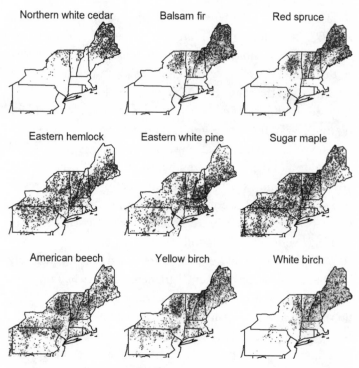

Figure 1. Abundance of nine of the most common tree species with primarily northern distributions in the nine northeastern United States. The gray scale of each dot on a map represents the relative abundance of the species (light gray = low, dark gray = high) in a plot where there was at least one tree of that species. Data come from 21,988 forest inventory plots in upland forest types sampled during the period from 1997 to 2012 by the US Forest Service Forest Inventory and Analysis program.

tree species in the nine northeastern states—red maple, sugar maple, eastern hemlock, white pine, and red oak—make up 50 percent of forest biomass in the region as a whole, and all five are common in both northern and southern forests.[4]

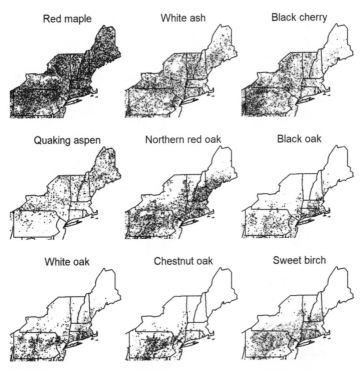

Figure 2. Abundance of nine of the most common tree species with primarily southern distributions in the nine northeastern United States. The gray scale of each dot on a map represents the relative abundance of the species (light gray = low, dark gray = high) in a plot where there was at least one tree of that species. Data come from 21,988 forest inventory plots in upland forest types sampled during the period from 1997 to 2012 by the US Forest Service Forest Inventory and Analysis program.

While the north/south climate differences clearly matter, the much more important environmental gradients in northeastern forests and indeed in most forests worldwide are due to finer-scale differences in soil moisture and soil fertility. There is a modest amount of regional variation in rainfall, mostly due to higher rainfall on the windward side of the Catskill, Adirondack, Green, and White Mountain ranges, and along the southern New England coast. But the most important differences in soil moisture are caused by local variation in soil depth, soil texture, and, to a lesser extent, topography, particularly north- versus south-facing slopes. Most northeastern tree species can be found across a very broad range of soil moisture availability, and the greatest impact of variation in soil moisture is on forest productivity and canopy height. Any hiker going up onto the thin soils of a rocky ridgeline in the Northeast will witness a steady progression of shorter and shorter canopy trees as a result of moisture limitation on growth of pretty much whatever trees species occur there. Measuring soil moisture availability in ecologically meaningful and accurate units turns out to be more challenging than you might imagine, since characterizing even a single growing season requires frequent monitoring to detect day-to-day variation in soil moisture. While the Northeast is generally considered a moist climate, for many species the critical factor is the severity of even very short-term droughts of a few weeks' duration. Those conditions are most common where the soils are either very thin, typically on hilltops and upper slopes, or very coarse, generally the sandy soils derived from glacial outwash. I suspect that beech is the most truly drought-sensitive of our upland forest species. While casual observation would classify it as a northern species, beech can be found as far south as Mexico, so temperature limitation is clearly not a factor in its scarcity in the dry, oak-dominated forests of southern New England.

As any gardener knows, plants need a long list of soil nutrients to thrive. For many years ecosystem scientists in the Northeast have focused on the availability of nitrogen as the most important nutrient limiting forest productivity. There are good reasons for this. Plants need to take up a great deal of both nitrogen and phosphorus on an annual basis, but the leaves of northeastern trees typically require ten to twenty times as much nitrogen as phosphorus. Since most of the Northeast was glaciated, its soils are young in geologic terms. Phosphorus tends to be slowly leached from surface soils on geologic timescales, so the young northeastern soils tend to be rich in phosphorus relative to demand for nitrogen. But this basic story is complicated by the fact that air pollution has been fertilizing northeastern forests for over fifty years at rates that are currently about six pounds of nitrogen per acre per year. Those forests have been surprisingly effective at retaining the nitrogen and protecting lakes and rivers from being acidified and enriched by it: so much so that ecosystem scientists are concerned about the effects of saturation of forest soils with excess nitrogen.[5] I have concluded that the continued preoccupation of ecosystem scientists with nitrogen cycling has more to do with how intellectually exciting nitrogen can be than with its importance in understanding the distribution and abundance of northeastern tree species. The rates of nitrogen cycling in forest soils are better thought of as a result of the composition of tree species than as a cause of their variation in distribution and abundance.

The study of calcium cycling is less exciting to most ecosystem scientists, in part because there are fewer steps in the cycle mediated by the biological activity of soil microbes. But there is ample evidence that the distributions of many tree species and also many shrubs, herbaceous species, and mosses vary systematically along gradients of soil calcium and the other base cations (positively charged ions of magnesium, sodium, and potassium) which are typically correlated with the concentration of calcium ions. Soils rich in these nutrients generally reflect

the weathering of glacial till derived from limestone and
marble bedrock. The highest concentrations tend to be in sites
directly underlain by that bedrock, but the glaciers were remarkably powerful bulldozers and smeared calcium-rich glacial till
often far afield of the underlying base-rich bedrock. Great
Mountain Forest, where, as noted, I have worked for many years,
is located on the much more acidic bedrock of Canaan Mountain in northwestern Connecticut. But the surrounding valley
floors are rich in limestone, and there are distinctive pockets of
base-rich soils even on top of the mountain. These were clearly formed from gravel ground up from the valley floor and left
behind on the mountaintop by the glaciers. The pockets are
easy to spot because a number of species of trees such as sugar
maple, shrubs like barberry, and otherwise rare herbaceous
species like maidenhair fern are more common there. As with
nitrogen, there is a vexing chicken/egg problem, since our work
at Great Mountain Forest shows that species do not just respond
to soil calcium and magnesium but actively alter the availability of those nutrients relative to the potential supply from the
weathering of the glacial till. But it seems clear to me that
variation in soil calcium plays a much larger role than variation
in nitrogen supply in the distribution and abundance of plants
in northeastern forests.

Gleason's individualistic principle is an intellectual
cousin of the notion of a species' niche. Niche theory goes
beyond and invokes species interactions and evolution to make
predictions about just how species are distributed across a range
of environmental conditions. In particular, ecologists have
emphasized the role of competition in limiting overlap in the
distributions of species along resource gradients. They have
focused even more attention on the theoretical power of competition to lead to exclusion of weaker competitors, thereby

reducing the potential biodiversity of a community. Yet biodiversity persists, and ecological theory is replete with potential mechanisms by which species manage to coexist. But that is not to say that the fundamental niche of a tree—i.e., the set of conditions under which it would occur in the absence of competition—is identical to the realized niche it is forced into given competition from neighbors of other species. There has been very little direct study of differences in the fundamental and realized niches of temperate trees. Colleagues and I have looked at this issue in just two studies, one for northern New England and one for southern New England and southeastern New York.[6] In each location our methods allowed us to compare the actual abundance of tree species along soil moisture and soil fertility gradients (their realized niches) with the conditions under which the species showed the greatest growth in the absence of competition (interpreted as an indication of their fundamental niches). Results were gratifyingly consistent between the two studies. In the absence of competition, the most shade-tolerant species, particularly sugar maple and beech, grow best in the sites where they are also most abundant (their fundamental and realized niches were identical). But the less shade-tolerant trees such as northern red oak, red maple, and eastern white pine are all most abundant on sites displaced toward the less fertile or drier end of the resource gradient than where they grow best in the absence of competition. So while tree species don't neatly and organically assemble themselves into discrete forest types, ecological interactions clearly play an important role in the distribution, abundance, and coexistence of the component species.

Niche theory offers one other important refinement to Gleason's individualistic principle. As humans, we intuitively apply value judgments to environmental resource gradients.

Places with high soil moisture and high soil fertility are implicitly assumed to be "better" sites since all plants need water and soil nutrients. But evolution doesn't make those judgments. So while competition appears to displace less shade-tolerant (less competitive?) trees to what we intuitively interpret as poorer sites, that is not to say that all species reach their highest potential growth on the richest sites. Beech trees reach their greatest abundance on soils low in available calcium, and our studies indicate that they also grow the best on those soils, even in the absence of competition. We have good evidence that beech trees actually act to maintain low concentrations of available calcium and nitrogen even on sites that would otherwise be more fertile.

So as I walk in the woods I find constantly changing local neighborhoods with different mixes of tree species. But I have never felt the need to put names or discrete boundaries on the communities I see around me. And even if I was so inclined, the currents outlined in the rest of this book would make it necessary to constantly revise and refine any such classification.

2

Charting a Course
Predicting Forest Futures

It's easy for ecologists to be a bit nostalgic about how simple and clean our models of forest dynamics were fifty years ago. Disturbances such as fires and windstorms were thought to be rare, and when they happened forests recovered through a process of succession with a predictable sequence of dominance by progressively more shade-tolerant tree species. Eugene Odum subtitled his most famous paper, cited over five thousand times and based on his presidential address at the 1966 Ecological Society of America meeting, with the assertion that "an understanding of ecological succession provides a basis for resolving man's conflict with nature." He argued that succession had a strategy, namely, "increased control of, or homeostasis with, the physical environment in the sense of achieving maximum protection from its perturbations."[1] There was such faith in the model that it was considered challenging in the 1970s to propose that there could be a variety of successional pathways involving different sequences of intermediate steps before reaching the inevitable climax community in any given environment (to say nothing of suggesting that forests might not ever reach equilibrium).

The earliest notions of plant succession dated from studies of vegetation development on progressively older sand dunes and new substrates revealed by the retreat of glaciers. The pioneer species on those sites pave the way for later stages by promoting soil development and retention of nutrients. Later stages repay the favor by creating conditions unfavorable for the pioneers. Early models of forest recovery following disturbance made similar assumptions that early successional trees created conditions at least suitable, if not actually needed by, later successional species. Frank Egler challenged this notion and in the 1950s famously issued a $10,000 wager—worth over $100,000 in today's dollars—that challenged ecologists to produce unambiguous evidence that the sequence of species was a "cause-and-effect phenomenon of ingoing and outgoing populations of plants." The alternative, now supported by abundant evidence, was that the observed succession of tree species was largely a product of differences in rates of dispersal and growth. The pioneers were species that produced copious numbers of small, widely dispersed seeds that allowed them to rapidly colonize recent disturbances and had very high growth rates in the full sun conditions present as a result of the disturbance. The late successional species were less effective at dispersal and slower growing in full sunlight but were capable of regenerating in deep shade. Needless to say, there was never a successful challenge to Egler's wager.[2]

The notion that tree species can be arrayed along a spectrum of shade tolerance was and is central to all ideas about forest succession, with the corollary that the most shade-tolerant species in a given environment will eventually dominate the climax community. Shade tolerance is determined by a broad suite of physiological and morphological traits, and those traits have trade-offs that make a particular strategy optimal for a particular light level. At the level of individual leaves, the metabolic and anatomical machinery needed to optimize growth under high light has high maintenance costs that preclude positive growth under low light. At the branch level, trees have flexible branch architecture and leaf orientation that allow them to optimize illumination of leaves without over-saturating them with light. But it is at the level of the tree crown that shade tolerance is most easily discerned. Henry Horn's classic work on the adaptive geometry of trees introduced the notion of the multilayered crowns of shade-tolerant trees. This translates into a very simple metric: the more shade tolerant a tree, the deeper its crown. I've always assumed this reflects the point at which it makes sense for a tree to slough its lowest branches. The more shade tolerant the tree, the longer it can hold on to its lowest branches before they no longer produce any net profit for the tree (carbohydrates that can be exported from the leaves to the rest of the tree). There is an important consequence to the deep crowns of shade-tolerant trees. They also cast the deepest shade in the understory (fig. 3).[3]

Despite the wealth of research on the many traits that define shade tolerance and the importance of shade tolerance for the successional status of a tree species, for most of the past century ecologists have used simple qualitative rankings of shade tolerance based on surveys of the opinions of field biologists, typically foresters. It is likely that those opinions were shaped by how frequently foresters saw seedlings and saplings in the shade of a forest understory. This begs the question of whether there is a more quantitative and functional way to assess shade tolerance. The simple answer to my mind is that tolerance implies ability to persist and that the best single measure of shade tolerance would be survival of seedlings and

saplings in deep shade regardless of how fast or slow they grow. The challenge has always been that accurate methods of measuring survival typically involve tracking thousands of seedlings and saplings over a period of many years. Twenty-five years ago Richard Kobe and Stephen Pacala devised an arcane but powerful statistical method that circumvented this limitation by taking advantage of the record of past growth recorded in the tree rings of live versus recently deceased saplings. That method, combined with other research at our study sites at Great Mountain Forest, provided quantitative estimates of expected survival of saplings as a function of variation in light level for all of the tree species at Great Mountain.[4]

Those estimates were a crucial part of our work to develop a new generation of computer model for forest dynamics, but they also provided two important lessons. The first was the realization that seedlings of all nine of the most common tree species at Great Mountain could survive in the shade cast by a closed canopy of their parents. But if the stand was invaded by a more shade-tolerant species, the new arrival would eventually cast deeper shade than the previous occupant could tolerate. This is a very simple but direct example of a competitive hierarchy in which the dominant species is the one that can tolerate depleting a critical resource to a level that others can't survive.[5] There was a satisfying twist for me in this story. It

---

Figure 3. Looking up through a canopy of northern red oak, but with a subcanopy and saplings of sugar maple and beech. A red oak canopy lets through almost twice as much sunlight as a canopy of beech or sugar maple, and red oak saplings can survive in the shade cast by adult red oaks. But those oak saplings can't survive very long in the deeper shade of the subcanopy and canopy of beech and maple. Photo by author.

certainly wasn't a story of parental nurturing: adult trees of a given species did not deliberately allow enough light to penetrate their canopies so that their seedlings could survive beneath them. But if the light level beneath the crown of an adult tree is determined by when the shade cast by higher branches is deep enough to make it slough its lowest branches, the fact that seedlings can survive at that light level suggests that a small seedling is functionally more shade tolerant than one of the lower branches of the parent tree.

This speaks to the inherent architectural and engineering cost of the branches needed to display leaves under low-light conditions. Light levels generally don't increase with height in the forest understory, at least until a sapling gets very tall. So as a seedling or sapling grows, its photosynthetic income per unit area of the leaves in its crown is constant, but the metabolic costs of producing and maintaining the branches needed to display those leaves are expected to rise. As a graduate student I was convinced that this would be a crucial aspect of the shade tolerance of sugar maple and beech saplings. In fact, those two species turned out to have simple but effective branch architecture that allowed them to minimize the metabolic costs of getting bigger in deep shade. But I remain convinced that the energetic cost of getting bigger in deep shade is a ubiquitous challenge that all trees face.[6]

The second lesson from this work, at least for me, was that no matter how well you think you understand a species or an ecosystem there are always surprises when you collect new data. The consensus from expert opinion has always been that sugar maple is a very shade-tolerant species. But the estimates from Great Mountain showed it to be only moderately tolerant. I considered this a direct affront to my earlier work on sugar maple in the Adirondacks. When new data challenge your expectations, it is probably human nature to first question the data—this was certainly my first inclination. But Kobe was confident enough in his methods that he sought a different explanation. Most of the soils at Great Mountain Forest are fairly acidic and low in calcium, and sugar maple is only moderately abundant on those soils. But it is far more common in the surrounding valleys, which have soils underlain by limestone that weathers to produce soils that are less acidic and have far higher availability of base cations like calcium. And sampling on those soils showed sugar maple seedlings to have far higher survival at low light. Prior to that work it was common to assume that shade tolerance was a fixed trait of a tree species, regardless of environment. We now realize that shade tolerance is a far more fluid trait that can vary with both climate and soil conditions.[7]

The notion of succession remains central to the way ecologists think about recovery of a forest following a major disturbance like a fire or clear-cutting. But succession theory makes only very general predictions about details of that recovery, and most of those details describe recovery of forest structure rather than composition. Although late successional forests are expected to be dominated by shade-tolerant tree species, the theory is silent on how many and which species can coexist in the climax community. And a large set of our native tree species are neither the highly shade-intolerant pioneers nor the highly shade-tolerant climax species. These intermediate species include some of the most common tree species in the region, such as red maple, white pine, yellow birch, white ash, and black cherry. The question of how those species fit in forest succession has revolved around the importance of smaller-scale disturbances that create openings in the forest canopy. A closed canopy of shade-tolerant trees intercepts roughly 98 percent of solar radiation over the growing season, leaving just 2 percent in the forest understory for seedlings and saplings. But the hole in the canopy left by the death of two to three adjacent adult trees can create spots in the understory with 10 to 15 percent of full sunlight, enough light for seedlings of the intermediate shade-tolerant species to survive and grow, if slowly. There was so much interest in the role of these gaps that ecologists began to treat the surrounding closed canopy as simply a background matrix of little interest. Indeed, the theoretical model most commonly invoked in those studies proposed that a forest could be considered a population of gaps that were "born" when a canopy tree or group of trees died and grew (negatively) as they shrank in size as surrounding trees filled them from the side. The gaps died (disappeared) when regeneration within the gap reached canopy size.[8]

I bought into these ideas wholeheartedly as a graduate student. But then I spent a summer walking transects through magnificent old-growth forests in the Upper Peninsula of Michigan, measuring gaps and the forest regeneration within them. I also spent a lot of time over the next few years figuring out how to quantify the obvious spatial variation in understory light levels in and around gaps in old-growth forests of the Adirondacks. And while I tried hard, I couldn't fit what I found within a neat theory of gap dynamics. The most common gaps in old-growth forests are formed by the death of a single large tree. At best they create small, transient patches of slightly higher light, water, and soil nutrients in the understory. But since the sun passes through the southern portion of the sky at our latitudes, the higher light is actually found underneath the canopy on the north edge of the gap.[9]

The upshot is that the most common gaps—those caused by the death of just one or two adjacent trees—are almost exclusively exploited by the most shade-tolerant tree species. My examination of the history of growth recorded in the tree rings of shade-tolerant trees that had successfully reached canopy size in old-growth forests in the Adirondacks showed that it often took one hundred years for a sugar maple or beech sapling to reach adulthood. Those hundred years as a sapling were typically punctuated by several distinct periods of rapid growth lasting fifteen to twenty years, presumably due to the presence of a canopy gap somewhere overhead, followed by periods of suppressed growth lasting twenty to thirty years after the gap closed and before another tree nearby died. This repeated pattern of release followed by suppression relies on the intrusion of higher light through a gap into the understory beneath the canopy across an arc from the northwest to the northeast of the edge of the gap itself. In effect, successfully reaching canopy size for a shade-tolerant sapling within an old-growth forest requires the very rare combination of several distinct periods of release when canopy trees nearby but southeast to southwest of the sapling die. The subsequent increase in light penetration on the north side of the gap allows the sapling to increase substantially in height. After two or three of these periods of release, it is poised beneath the canopy of the tree directly overhead. There, if it is lucky and the tree above it dies within the next decade or two, it will be able to reach the canopy before surrounding trees can close the gap from the side.[10]

This work led me to conclude that while tree species could be arrayed along a continuum defined by survival of their seedlings and saplings in deep shade, in reality there was a qualitative threshold that a species needed to meet to be considered truly shade tolerant. This threshold is defined by the ability to have a reasonable chance of surviving the period of suppression beneath a closed canopy before the next gap forms nearby. I tend to use surviving thirty years of suppression as a rough benchmark. On that basis, only beech and hemlock—and sugar maple on less acidic soils—would be considered shade tolerant at Great Mountain Forest, with more than 75 percent of saplings expected to survive thirty years of suppression. For the rest of the species there, including some like yellow birch that are traditionally considered moderately shade tolerant, fewer than a quarter would be expected to survive that long in deep shade. If a species meets the threshold, there is still a range of strategies and traits that determine how a shade-tolerant species reaches adulthood in the absence of a notable disturbance. For example, the race to the canopy between beech and sugar maple saplings in an old-growth forest is the plant world's version of the classic contest between the tortoise and the hare. Beech, as the tortoise, has a suite of physiological and architectural traits that allow it to continue to grow slowly but incrementally in deep shade, but it has only a modest increase in growth when a gap forms above it. Sugar maple for all intents and purposes halts vertical growth when suppressed but is able to build up leaf display rapidly once a gap forms with a correspondingly faster vertical growth in the gap than beech.

But in the case of the much larger set of tree species that can't exploit these short-lived, small, single-tree gaps, their dynamics are inextricably tied to traits that determine their responses to disturbances that kill reasonably large numbers of canopy trees. The few true pioneers like paper birch and trembling aspen represent one extreme: adapted to only large, catastrophic disturbances, particularly fire and clear-cutting. The remaining species employ a variety of strategies to exploit less extreme disturbances. Red maple is the most common tree in the eastern United States in large part because it can grow everywhere, from swamps to dry, rocky ridgetops. But it also has a regeneration strategy that is successful in a wide range of severities and types of disturbance. If cut down, it sprouts pro-lifically from its stump. As an adult it produces frequent and reliably large crops of wind-dispersed seeds. The seeds are small enough that they don't attract too much attention from rodent seed predators but large enough to establish large cohorts of new seedlings throughout the understory every few years. Those seedlings don't meet my threshold to be considered truly shade tolerant but instead have a go-for-broke strategy of maximizing height growth as a seedling and small sapling, at the expense of a high mortality rate if the canopy doesn't open up overhead within ten to fifteen years. In effect, they maintain a constantly replenished pool of what foresters call advance regeneration, that is, seedlings and saplings ready to respond when a suffi-ciently large opening forms in the canopy.

Yellow birch offers an example of a very different strategy, especially in its response to windstorms. This starts with the ability of adults to ride out even fairly extreme winds, losing branches but keeping enough of a canopy to provide a good crop of very small, widely wind-dispersed seeds the next year. Those seeds are even smaller than red maple and do best when they land on bare soil. Luckily, windstorms create just the right substrate on the large tip-up mounds formed when trees are uprooted. And since the tops of those mounds are often one to two meters above the forest floor, new yellow birch seedlings have a head start on some of the advance regeneration of other species established before the storm. Yellow birch is so success-ful following major windstorms that whenever I encounter it in abundance I expect that most of them are the same age and date from a single large storm sometime in the past few hundred years. Unfortunately, large yellow birch trees are prone to heart rot, so it is rare to be able to core the trees and use tree rings to determine the exact year of the storm.

One of the advantages of working in temperate forests like those of the northeastern United States is that there are few enough tree species that ecologists have been able to characterize the basic natural history of virtually all of them.[11] Turning those individual life histories into predictions of the dynamics of the ensemble of species that make up any particular forest community has been the province of computer simulation models. The earliest forest models ran on mainframe computers and were probably motivated as much by a desire to demonstrate the potential role of computer models in ecology as by particular hypotheses about forest succession. As a graduate student and young field biologist I was not impressed by those first attempts. They made simplifying assumptions that omitted most of the rich ecological detail and natural history that I was interested in. For example, they ignored the enormous spatial and temporal variation in understory light levels created when canopy trees died. More fundamentally, the parameters and mathematical functions in the models often had no direct relationship to anything you could actually measure in the field. As a result the parameter values were set by expert opinion; typically the person who had developed the model was the sole expert. This created the potential for the parameters to be tuned to predict expected results. To be fair, the modelers were probably (and justifiably) frustrated by these sorts of criticisms, since the most basic goal of any model is to provide a simplified description of the system. And while models make quantitative predictions, to most modelers the exact predictions are less valuable than the ability of a model to assess the logical consequences of and relative importance of the various mechanisms incorporated in the model. As an example, forest ecologists invest a disproportionate amount of their field research efforts in the study of tree seedlings. This makes intuitive sense but also reflects the ease of experimentally manipulating and measuring seedlings versus manipulating and monitoring adult trees. But you need to embed those seedling dynamics in a model of the whole life history of the tree and the forest to assess how important seedlings really are.

Pacala changed my attitudes about models almost thirty years ago when he convinced me that it was possible both to incorporate the messy spatial heterogeneity I was interested in and to design field studies that would yield the actual functions and parameters a model needed. That first model, developed in the early 1990s with John Silander, Pacala's colleague at the University of Connecticut, was based on five years of intensive field research at Great Mountain Forest, including the doctoral theses of six students at the University of Connecticut.[12] In the lexicon of forest models, it had two distinctive and at that time novel features. The first was that it was explicitly demographic: it tracked the spatial locations and birth, growth, and death of all individual seedlings, saplings, and adult trees rather than simply track changes in the total numbers of individuals by size class and species across a plot. The second was that it incorporated spatial variability in two key ecological processes. Almost the entire computational burden in the model (written initially in the C programming language and run under the MS-DOS operating system on a single IBM personal computer) was devoted to characterizing the effects of canopy trees and gaps on spatial variation in the understory light levels experienced by seedlings and saplings. This variation in light was paired with field studies of the growth of saplings as a function of light levels and used the field methods developed by Kobe and Pacala to link sapling growth to survival. In this way the model captured what I felt were the critical details of the successional processes by which seedlings and saplings responded to canopy tree mortality and disturbance.

The other novel spatial feature of the model was based on methods that Eric Ribbens and Pacala developed to measure the effective dispersal of seedlings around parent trees. As I've mentioned, differences in dispersal ability have long been assumed to be part of the suite of traits that determine whether a species is a pioneer or a climax species. But given the dearth of research on actual dispersal distances for tree seeds and seedlings, previous models had just assumed that forests were uniformly blanketed with seeds, regardless of where the parents were.[13]

Even that first and relatively simple model predicted highly complex patterns of succession. Far from the deterministic sequence of species replacement envisioned by early succession theory, the model predicted wildly varying patterns depending on initial conditions and depending even on the exact spatial distributions of the trees in a stand at the start of a simulation. A corollary of this is that the response of a forest to a disturbance was highly dependent on the specific mix of species and tree sizes present at the time of disturbance, with many different possible successional trajectories. This kind of dependence on initial conditions is in fact one of the defining features of chaos theory in mathematics. More practically, foresters have long recognized that they can redirect the next hundred years of stand development through actions that promote regeneration of one species or another immediately after a disturbance like logging. And while the composition predicted by the model in the absence of any notable disturbance would eventually roughly stabilize, that stage could take over a millennium to materialize.

After we published results of the field research and presented the original model in a paper in 1996, that research group split up, and Pacala and Silander went off to work on new questions in other ecosystems.[14] But I had found in Great Mountain Forest what I considered to be an ideal research site. It had been managed as a sustainable working forest since 1909 by three generations of the Childs family and had been actively supporting research on forestry and ecology for much of that time. There was also a wonderful, if rustic, camp on the property where research assistants and graduate students could live during the summer. And it was close enough to the Cary Institute that time-sensitive samples could be ferried to my lab easily. Over the next decade colleagues and I expanded our field research to consider a host of other processes we thought might need to be incorporated in any model of forest dynamics, including nutrient cycling (with the graduate students Adrien Finzi, Natasja van Gestel, and Feike Dijksra and the postdoc Seth Bigelow), competition between adult trees (with Michael Papaik), the impacts of small mammals and white-tailed deer (with Jackie Schnurr and Chris Tripler), invasive tree species (with the postdocs Patrick Martin and Lorena Gómez-Aparicio), and forest pests and pathogens (with Erika Latty and Radka Wildova).

While all of that work was focused on topics that would be considered strictly the province of forest ecology, the highest and best use of the approach we developed may well be its application in silviculture. Decades of forestry research had been devoted to the development of models to predict forest regrowth following clear-cutting. These "growth and yield" models were central to economic forecasting and determination of sustainable yield in landscapes managed through clear-cutting. But between concerns over the environmental effects of clear-cutting and developments in both the economics and technology of harvesting trees selectively, many foresters were looking for models that could be used to explore alternatives to clear-cutting. The ability to capture the spatial heterogeneity created by a wide range of levels of canopy disturbance meant that our approach could be easily adapted to simulate a wide range of partial harvesting strategies. Support for research on new approaches to forest management in the northeastern US has declined precipitously over the past twenty to thirty years. But Canadians take forest management very seriously, in part because, in contrast to the United States, so much of their working forestland base is publicly owned. David Coates in British Columbia and Christian Messier in Quebec have been strong proponents of the need for new ecological perspectives on forest management. Both share my commitment to strengthening the linkage between modeling and field research, and my collaborations with them have had an enormous impact on my thinking about both forest dynamics and options for new forest management in the northeastern United States.[15]

The perspectives and approach that grew out of my early collaboration with Pacala and Silander have shaped much of my research since then. The original model we developed has long since been discarded in favor of a far more flexible and powerful modeling framework that can accommodate a wide range of research.[16] When we now use the model to explore issues like the potential impact of climate change on forests across the eastern United States, we simulate thousands of stands as a representative sample of current forest conditions and, still using personal computers but large clusters of them now, generate terabytes of detailed output on how those stands change over time. It's easy to get lost and revel in the detail, and the projections made by any model are always more beguiling than they should be.

The most noteworthy impact of work with the model, at least for me, has been in how it has shaped the way I think about how forests work. I've already admitted to my preoccupation with spatial variability within forests. Traditionally, when ecologists sample a forest, they arbitrarily stake out the boundaries of a plot and average over the variability of whatever they are measuring within the plot. The alternative is what I think of as a neighborhood approach. As I walk through the woods I can pause at any location and scan the distribution of the trees in the immediate neighborhood. Depending on what I'm interested in—whether the number or growth of saplings of a given species, the availability of some resource like light or a soil nutrient at that exact location, or the abundance and activity of a small mammal—the size of the neighborhood I need to consider will differ. And regardless of what ecological attribute I'm measuring, the spatial arrangement of the species and sizes of trees around that particular point will be one of the most important factors to consider. There are certainly physical effects of the underlying soil substrate, but even in the soil most of the attributes that matter to the trees are strongly influenced by the configuration of the trees in the immediate neighborhood.

I think of these effects in terms of the overlapping ecological footprints of individual trees (figs. 4, 5). Leaf litterfall is a prime example. It is a critical step in nutrient cycling since it represents a large return of nutrients to the soil each year. The distribution of leaf litter around individual trees varies predictably as a function of the size and shape of the leaves and the force of wind required to separate leaves from twigs. Of the six species shown in figure 4, red oak and beech trees produce total quantities of leaf litter that are similar to the other species, but their large leaves are distributed across a much larger area. Both species are in the same family (Fagaceae), and species in that family tend to hold on to their leaves due to incomplete abscission layers. As a result, their leaves tend to be released only under stronger winds than the other species. The species also differ in the chemistry of those leaves, and the aggregate effect of the species on soil nutrient availability (see fig. 5).

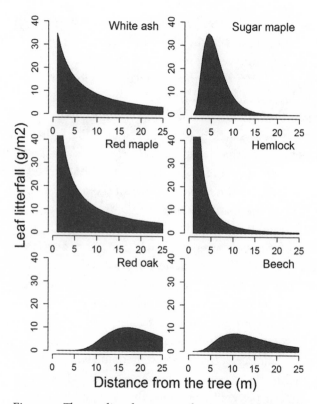

Figure 4. The predicted amount of autumn leaf litterfall as a function of distance from a single thirty centimeter diameter tree within a forest. Litterfall also varies as a function of direction due to prevailing winds during the fall, and these figures are plotted for the direction of maximum dispersal distance (generally east to northeast of the tree). Data redrawn from Seth W. Bigelow and Charles D. Canham, "Litterfall as a Niche Construction Process in a Northern Hardwood Forest," *Ecosphere* 6 (2015): 117, http://dx.doi.org/10.1890/ES14-00442.1.

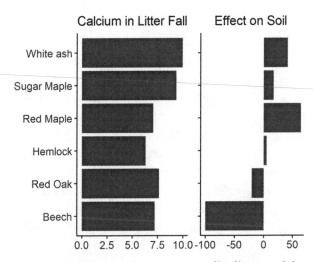

Figure 5. Variation in calcium content of leaf litter, and the relative effect of the different species on calcium concentrations in soil beneath their crowns. Units in the panel on the left are in milligrams of calcium per gram of dried leaf litter. Figure for calcium in litterfall redrawn from data in Bigelow and Canham (2015) (cited in the caption for figure 4). Figure for species effects redrawn from results in Seth W. Bigelow and Charles D. Canham, "Neighborhood-Scale Analyses of Non-Additive Species Effects on Cation Concentrations in Forest Soils," *Ecosystems* 20 (2017): 1351–63.

The patterns are particularly striking for the availability and cycling of calcium and nitrogen. White ash and sugar maple are calcicoles—most abundant on soils high in available calcium—and their leaf litter reflects this, returning large amounts of calcium back to the soil each fall. The two calcifuges, red oak and beech, have the opposite pattern. They occur on soils with characteristically low available calcium and produce leaf litter that has lower concentrations of calcium. The six species tend to occur on soils that differ in the amount of calcium in the parent material from which the soils weathered. But for any given amount of calcium in the parent material—a form that is still bound up in the soil minerals and is not available to the plants—the species also have dramatically different aggregate effects on the amount of available calcium (shown as "effect on soil" in fig. 5). Presence of beech in a neighborhood dramatically depresses the amount of calcium available in the soil, regardless of how much was potentially available in the parent material. The same is true to a lesser extent for red oak. Red maple, white ash, and sugar maple have the opposite effect—maintaining relatively high amounts of available calcium in the soil regardless of the concentration of calcium in the parent material. More critically, there is an antagonistic effect on calcium availability of the presence of beech or red oak in a neighborhood containing species like sugar maple and white ash, reducing calcium below what would be expected from simply the weighted average of the effects of the different species. This is exacerbated by the wide distribution of leaf litter of beech and red oak.

Over the years colleagues and I have looked at a wide range of ecological processes from this neighborhood perspective. A number of general conclusions have emerged from that work. The first is that forest neighborhoods are very local. For most of the processes we have studied, the effective neighborhood radius around any particular point of interest is less than twenty meters. With a few notable exceptions two trees separated by more than twenty meters are ignorant of each other's existence; or at least their interactions are minor enough to be ignored by a forest ecologist.[17]

Another point is that it is critically important whether the effects of neighboring trees are simply additive or whether they interact positively or negatively. For example, falling leaves of sugar maples have relatively high concentrations of nitrogen and decompose and release that nitrogen rapidly when they hit the forest floor. Beech leaves have lower nitrogen by the time they are dropped from the tree and decompose and release that nitrogen much more slowly. So stands dominated by sugar maple generally have higher rates of cycling of nitrogen through the soil whereas neighborhoods dominated by beech have slower turnover of nitrogen in the soil. As described above, the same pattern holds for the effects of these two species on soil calcium. It is common for the two species to occur together within a neighborhood, and, as you'd expect, nitrogen and calcium cycling rates are generally intermediate when both species are present. If the effects of the two species were additive, then the average nutrient cycling rate across a stand would be a simple function of the total numbers and sizes of the trees of the two species. As the composition of the stand changed over time, you could predict changes in the nutrient cycling rates by simply knowing changes in the average relative abundance of the species in the stand.

There is evidence, however, for both nitrogen and calcium cycling that the presence of a beech tree in the immediate neighborhood depresses the otherwise stronger effect of a nearby sugar maple tree.[18] There are many possible mechanisms for nonadditive effects such as these. Regardless of the exact mechanism, if species effects are nonadditive, then predicting changes over time in a broad range of ecosystem attributes requires knowledge not just of the average abundance of the species across a stand but also of the exact spatial arrangement of trees of different species and sizes within the stand. This is not an idea that is comforting to most ecosystem scientists because it implies that all of the messy species interactions and unpredictable disturbance events that determine changes in the actual spatial arrangements of trees within a stand need to be taken into account. More fundamentally, it implies that the dynamics of most ecosystem processes will take on the stochastic and almost infinitely variable successional sequences that our models predict for tree species dynamics. This is a very far cry from the simple, deterministic, and homeostatic view of succession driving ecosystem development that Odum envisioned fifty years ago.

3

Home Port

The Ebb and Flow of Presettlement Forests

While notions of steady state have only a tenuous hold on the way ecologists currently think of eastern forests, it has been much harder to let go of the idea of a presettlement baseline against which to measure changes in northeastern forests over the past four hundred years and where they are headed in the next few centuries. The settlement in this case is by Europeans and ignores thousands of years of occupation of the region by Native Americans following retreat of the Pleistocene glaciers. But if we are going to use the condition of forests four hundred years ago as a meaningful baseline, it is important to have a clear picture of their ebb and flow. While studies of the reestablishment of northeastern forests following retreat of the glaciers date back almost a century, that topic has taken on added significance for what it can tell us about the ways our forests will respond to future climate change. And the nature of the pre-European landscape remains a touchstone for debates about conservation biology and forest management in the region.

Much of what we know about forest history during the millennia prior to European settlement comes from the work of palynologists, members of a branch of the field of paleoecology in which sediment cores are extracted from the bottoms of lakes. The scientists then spend a year or more carefully extracting, counting, and identifying the different species of pollen grains preserved at different depths. Radiocarbon dating of the sediments provides a way to document the abundance of tree species present in the surrounding landscape at the time the sediments were formed.[1]

Those studies paint a remarkably detailed picture of the waves of migration of individual tree species back into the northeastern and upper midwestern states. Much of that pattern is attributed to climate change since the end of the Pleistocene and to a lesser extent to limitations in innate rates of tree dispersal and migration. Spruces, firs, and then pines were typically the first trees to become abundant, at least in terms of the pollen they deposited in the bottoms of lakes. But at least trace amounts of pollen of most of the modern genera of tree species can be detected within one to two thousand years following retreat of the glaciers. A notable exception was the American chestnut, which arrived in southern New England only around three thousand years ago—and then was decimated by chestnut blight during the past century. It was assumed that its arrival was delayed by slow rates of dispersal of its large seeds, but more recent studies attribute its arrival to the timing of an increase in precipitation in the region.[2]

It is typical for palynologists to identify distinct time periods dominated by different mixes of tree species, mark the dates of the transitions between those stages, and then attempt to explain the variations between those periods based on either the known, modern climate responses of the tree species or

independently measured "proxies" of past climates. Those proxies have become increasingly sophisticated as a result of the
effort to understand just how variable past climates have been.
Indeed, the pollen record for the past twelve thousand years
suggests enormous fluctuations in the abundance of tree species,
with different stories at different locations. Of the hundreds of
lakes in the northeastern United States that have been studied,
I picked the patterns at two of them, as much for my love of
their location as for their representativeness. Heart Lake in the
Adirondacks is known to generations of hikers as the stepping-
off point for a trek up Mount Marcy. Donald Whitehead and
Stephen Jackson published their study of this and three other
Adirondack lakes in 1990.[3] It's a deep lake by Adirondack
standards—over 13 meters at its deepest point—and the sediments date back to almost twelve thousand years before present.
The pollen profile in those sediments shows the expected
sequence of early abundance of pollen of spruce, fir, and pines
(fig. 6). By ten thousand (radiocarbon) years ago birches became
a ubiquitous feature of the landscape, although the birch genus
(*Betula*) includes tundra and boreal shrubs, and the birch pollen grains in the older sediments at Heart Lake were of the
smaller grain size typical of those shrubs. Hemlock and beech
provide a striking demonstration of the degree to which two
species that are commonly linked in modern-day forests of the
region can have very disparate histories. I assume that the
resurgence of spruce and fir in the past two thousand to four
thousand years at this elevation (661 meters) reflects the current
abundance of red spruce and balsam fir in low-elevation forests
as well as their dominance in the subalpine forests of the surrounding High Peaks.

Sutherland Pond, 269 kilometers south of Heart Lake, is
nestled in Black Rock Forest in the Hudson Highlands, one of

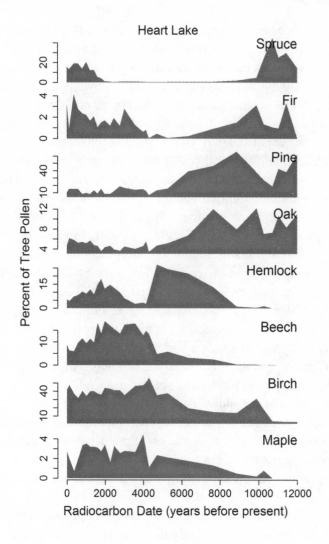

Heart Lake

Percent of Tree Pollen

Spruce
Fir
Pine
Oak
Hemlock
Beech
Birch
Maple

Radiocarbon Date (years before present)

my favorite places to ramble as a teenager. The lake yielded over ten meters of sediment cores. The deepest sediments indicate open tundra vegetation before 12,600 (radiocarbon) years ago but then a rapid rise in the abundance of spruce, fir, and pine pollen (fig. 7). The author of the study, Terryanne Maenza-Gmelch, was extraordinarily diligent in sampling thin slices of the sediment, yielding a very high temporal resolution to the reconstruction.[4] The early pulse of birch pollen presumably reflects the period known as the Younger Dryas, a 1,000-year-long period of abruptly cooler weather after the initial warming at the end of the Pleistocene. But after that, oak rapidly becomes and remains the dominant tree pollen in Sutherland Pond sediments for the past 8,000 years. Grains of charcoal are common in the sediments throughout the period of oak dominance, suggesting that fires were common in the surrounding landscape.

I have stared at these and many other palynologists' diagrams and find them fascinating and a source of endless speculation. I can never quite figure out, however, exactly how the different time periods are delineated or what to make of the incredible zigzags in the abundance of pollen over time for any one group of species. It seems clear that the broad patterns of change in species abundance do reflect changes in climate, and we have learned a great deal about how variable the climate of the northeastern United

Figure 6. Changes in the relative abundance of genera of tree species over the past twelve thousand years at Heart Lake in the Adirondack Mountains of New York. Figure redrawn from data from Donald R. Whitehead and Stephen T. Jackson, "The Regional Vegetational History of the High Peaks (Adirondack Mountains) New York," *New York State Museum Bulletin*, no. 478. (1990): ISBN 1-55557-195-6. Data downloaded from http://apps.neotomadb.org/explorer/.

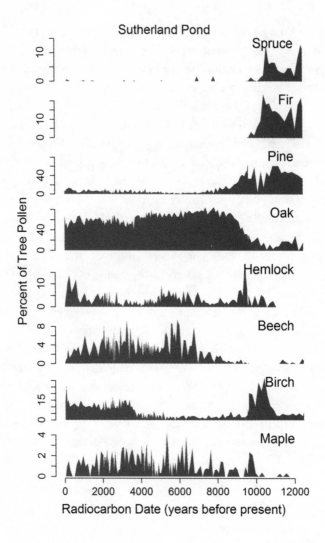

States has been over the past fourteen thousand years. But I see two other lessons (and limitations) in the data. The first is a reaffirmation that communities are transient assemblages of species mixes that are in constant flux in space and time. Jackson has been eloquent on this point.[5] A corollary is a confirmation of the principle that species are distributed individualistically in space and time rather than in distinct, persistent communities or vegetation types. Thus I see little reason to be surprised by the appearance of new mixes of tree species over the past few centuries or overly concerned about the disappearance of a particular mix of species that was present prior to settlement.

Paleoecologists are used to thinking in timescales of millennia and often argue that forests are in approximate equilibrium with climate on those timescales. But the second lesson I take from their work is that there is little reason to believe that the abundance of any single species closely tracks even the relatively modest rates of climate change that occurred during those twelve thousand years. The pollen record is simply not precise enough to allow us to assess exactly how much of a lag there might be in the responses of different tree species to climate change.

To my mind the most striking result from the work of the palynologists is evidence of a widespread, remarkably rapid decline in the abundance of hemlock pollen in lake sediments roughly fifty-five hundred years ago. Margaret Davis, one of the

Figure 7. Changes in the relative abundance of genera of tree species over the past twelve thousand years at Sutherland Pond in the Hudson Highlands of New York. Figure redrawn from data reported by Terryanne E. Maenza-Gmelch, "Late-Glacial—Early Holocene Vegetation, Climate, and Fire at Sutherland Pond, Hudson Highlands, Southeastern New York, U.S.A.," *Canadian Journal of Botany* 75 (1997): 431–39. Data downloaded from http://apps.neotomadb.org/explorer/.

pioneers of this branch of ecology, proposed in 1981 that the decline represented the first (and only) occurrence in that twelve-thousand-year record of a widespread, synchronous decimation of a native tree species due to a pest or pathogen. Other studies have challenged this hypothesis and have attributed the dramatic decline to climate change, particularly a long period of notably dry climate that began around the same time and persisted for several thousand years. I personally find the evidence for both explanations inconclusive, but this has more to do with the limitations of ascribing causation to such long-ago events. Increasingly sophisticated methods of reconstructing past climates and dating the spatial variation in hemlock decline have not fully resolved the debate.[6] Regardless of the exact cause or causes, the most important lesson from my perspective is that recovery of hemlock populations at any given location took anywhere from centuries to several thousand years. Moreover, there is evidence in some pollen cores, including Heart Lake (see fig. 6), to suggest that the recovery peaked several thousand years ago and that hemlock abundance has been gradually declining since then.

There could be many causes for the slow recovery and subsequent decline of hemlock, including several thousand years of an unusually dry climate in southern New England. But our analyses with demographic models suggest a far simpler if perhaps less likely explanation. When we simulate a single episode of massive, 95 percent hemlock mortality, particularly in stands where a close competitor like beech is present, it can take a thousand years, that is, four to five generations, for hemlock to regain its former abundance as it claws back space in the canopy from its strongest competitors.[7] Thus, regardless of the cause of the original decline it is not unreasonable to expect such events to have legacies that last for many generations. This is not a comforting thought given the litany of introduced pests and pathogens that have decimated so many northeastern tree species in the last one hundred years.

The nature and extent of Native Americans' impacts on northeastern forests during the ten thousand years before European settlement have been debated for decades. Despite increasingly sophisticated methods, I suspect that anthropologists and ecologists will never be able to put to rest arguments about just how much of a role early human hunters played in the extinction of so much of the wildly diverse Pleistocene megafauna of which mastodons are just one of the largest and most widely known representatives. Evidence suggests that northeastern agriculture and its associated land clearing became extensive only late in the postglacial period, with cultivation of maize appearing roughly five hundred years before the arrival of Europeans. The common assumption is that land clearing for cultivation was limited to the best soils, typically on river floodplains and lake deltas. Attempts to reconstruct forest conditions at the time of European settlement in proximity to previous Native American settlements have concluded that the percentage of land cleared was in the single digits, and only then very close to known settlement sites. Those studies, however, suggest that Native Americans had effects on forest composition and structure across much more of the landscape. For example, there have been suggestions that there was active forest management in the form of propagating species of nut-bearing trees like the hickories and oaks with particularly palatable acorns. A number of authors have also suggested that fire was deliberately used by Native Americans, especially in the drier oak/hickory forests, as a way to maintain a more open canopy that provided better habitat for hunting. And while there is ample evidence of charcoal in many lake sediments, there is

Figure 8. White pines along a lakeshore in an old-growth forest in the Adirondack Mountains of New York. The soils along the shore are sandy, and this stand may well have originated following a windstorm or lightning-caused fire two centuries ago. The sound of wind through a white pine canopy is, along with the call of the common loon, one of the most distinctive sounds of the northern forest. Photo by author.

little direct evidence of how those fires were started. To my mind one of the most compelling arguments for invoking a Native American role in the presettlement fire regime is that natural sources of ignition such as dry lightning are uncommon in northeastern forests, unlike the many forests of the western United States where lightning strikes and fire are ever-present.[8]

My best guess is that in the cooler, moister climates of northern New England, however, fires were limited to only the driest soils and did not require Native Americans as a source of ignition. Such sites would have been found on the thin soils of rocky mountaintops or at lower elevations on the unique bedrock "pavement barrens" as well as on the more common but still scattered deep, sandy glacial deposits of outwash plains and eskers. Pines would have been the likeliest occupants of those sites, with white pine and red pine on the better sites with less frequent but more severe fires and jack pine under more extreme conditions with more frequent fires (fig. 8). In contrast, the vast northern forest appears to have been far less fire-prone, at least before European settlement and the slash left behind by waves of logging.

But if fire was not a major disturbance in those northern forests, wind certainly could have been. My first research project as a graduate student was to try to document the frequency of catastrophic windstorms in the presettlement forests of Wisconsin. Accounts by early explorers of vast swaths of forests in the upper Midwest that had been toppled by winds were disturbing enough to potential settlers that surveyors sent out by the US General Land Office to map the new territories were ordered to also map the distribution of those blowdowns. I spent a summer in the Wisconsin state archives poring over the original township maps from the 1830s. The size and shapes of the blowdowns recorded by the earliest surveyors suggest that thunderstorm downbursts and tornadoes were the primary cause, at least in the continental climates of the upper Midwest. Settlers in New England would have been more familiar with the threats from coastal hurricanes. But it turns out that truly catastrophic wind disturbance is a very rare phenomenon in either the upper Midwest or the Northeast and occurred on timescales measured in thousands rather than hundreds of years.[9] Much more common would have been less intense but still damaging winds generated by severe low-pressure systems, either tropical hurricanes or extra-tropical cyclones formed in mid-latitude regions. Interest in these intermediate disturbances, at least from the perspective of ecological theory, has focused on whether—by opening up the forest canopy and providing conditions suitable for regeneration of less shade-tolerant species—they act as a mechanism to maintain species diversity. My colleagues' and my analyses suggest that in most cases these storms largely just accelerate dominance by late-successional, shade-tolerant tree species like beech. This outcome is likely because the storms generally topple the largest canopy trees and leave understory trees and saplings, which are typically dominated by shade-tolerant species, to benefit. These storms do clearly benefit some of the intermediate shade-tolerant species. Yellow birch, perhaps the best example, survives storms better than most, is a prolific, frequent producer of light, wind-dispersed seeds that scatter widely after a storm, and is ideally adapted to germinate and get established on the tip-up mounds produced when trees are uprooted.

While pollen in lake sediments provides our best picture of changes in forests over the span of postglacial history, our most precise snapshot of forest conditions at the time of European settlement comes from a very different source. Farmers followed the first wave of explorers and fur trappers in the region. They needed title to their land, and those deeds required surveys. By the middle of the eighteenth century it was routine for surveyors to record at least the species if not also the size of the nearest "witness" tree to the corners of a lot. In many cases they would also record a general description of the tree species encountered along a lot line. The surveyors were not botanists and recorded species by common names that often lumped ecologically dissimilar species such as sugar maple and red maple. I confess that I still have trouble telling red oak from black oak unless acorns are present, and in many of the surveys it's not possible to reliably distinguish between a half dozen or more species of oaks. Hickories (genus *Carya*) are not found in Europe, and the earliest surveyors appear to have referred to them often as walnuts. But ecologists have invested a lot of effort in resolving these issues, and the level of detail that can be recovered from these early surveys is quite remarkable. This work also requires an extraordinary level of patience and determination in digging out and transcribing the surveyors' handwritten field notes. The earliest surveys in the northeastern United States were typically done at the level of individual towns or on specific land grants or patents issued first by the English Crown and, after the Revolution, by the new republic. In new territories opening up from Ohio westward survey methods were standardized beginning in 1785. A regular grid of one-mile-square sections was organized into thirty-six-square-mile townships, a pattern familiar to anyone looking down from an airplane over the midwestern United States. Those methods formalized the recording of witness trees in a way that allows even more precise estimates of the distribution and abundance of tree species.[10]

Witness trees paint a remarkably consistent picture of northeastern forests at the time of European settlement. Beech was the overwhelmingly dominant tree species in the northernmost forests, ranging from northern New Hampshire across northern New York, through the Finger Lakes and the Catskills, and into the Allegheny plateau of Pennsylvania. For much of that region hemlock would have been the second most abundant species, with maples (predominantly sugar maple) more abundant on the better soils. But all evidence suggests that the early- to mid-successional tree species that dominate our current northern forests, species like the aspens, paper birch, red maple, white ash, and black cherry, were rare in the presettlement landscape. In effect, given the very modest levels of disturbance by Native Americans and windstorms, the northern forest region appears to have been a largely unbroken old-growth forest of late-successional, shade-tolerant tree species. Recent analyses of northern forests of the Midwest that take advantage of the more precise witness tree data indicate that those forests would have fit our expectation of forests with enormous, majestic trees and very high biomass.[11]

There appears to have been more variability in the oak-hickory forests of southern New England, although oaks, like beech in the north, were the overwhelmingly dominant tree species. Given the likelihood that fire, at least in the form of low-intensity ground fires, appears to have been common in that landscape, it is harder for me to visualize just what those forests looked like. Again, it seems likely that enormous trees were present since the thick bark of large oak trees tends to protect them from fire. Early botanical explorers described fairly open understories in oak forests. But oak-hickory forests in southern New England are often found on very thin, rocky soils subject to a lot of drought stress, and we have little way of knowing the structure and biomass of those forests with any precision. Despite this uncertainty, the forces I discuss below suggest that it is the oak-hickory forests that have drifted the farthest from their presettlement mooring and are the least likely to return to home port.

4

Legacies of Agricultural Clearing and Early Logging

The picture that emerges from the postglacial history of northeastern forests is one of constant change in both climate and tree species. But nothing in that twelve-thousand-year record compares to the pace of change in the past four hundred years. The waves of transformation of the northeastern landscape by early agriculture and logging have been well documented by historians and ecologists. In many ways that history is a testament to the resilience of our forests. The clearing of as much as 85 percent of southern New England by 1900 and the subsequent recovery of forests to levels that now approach 70 percent of the landscape are arguably one of the great conservation success stories of the past century. That most of the recovery occurred because of benign neglect by humans, allowing trees to do the job of reforesting on their own, does not diminish its importance. And the depredations of early logging in northern forests in the last half of the nineteenth century at a time of growing environmental consciousness played a major role in the emergence of

modern forest management in this country. Those concerns
were also critical in what is just as arguably the single greatest
conservation success of that era: the passage in 1894 of an
amendment to the New York State constitution (now known as
Article XIV) that protects public lands in the Adirondack and
Catskill Mountains as "forever wild." Today, the more than 1.2
million hectares of forest preserves in the Adirondacks and
Catskills represent not only over 70 percent of the forests in the
Northeast that are legally protected from logging but also the
largest wilderness areas east of the Boundary Waters of Minnesota and north of the Everglades.

The broad outlines of these stories of intensive logging
and clearing of forest for agriculture followed by eventual reforestation fit the ecological model of disturbance and recovery.
Yet closer examination shows that it is more apt to describe
these transformations as setting many of our forests off on new
courses, courses whose legacies could persist for at least the
next two to three centuries. And even where the natural sequence of recovery hasn't been altered, the sheer magnitude of
the replacement of presettlement, old-growth forests with young
forests means that the dynamics of forest succession triggered
by the past three hundred years of land use will be the single
most important cause of change in the broad features of northeastern forests over at least the next one hundred years. After
that, climate change will set a new and much more uncertain
course. The exact direction of the changes will reflect a whole
host of human impacts (as I discuss in the rest of the book), but
the underlying dynamics of forest succession are inexorable
and will shape the landscape for centuries to come.

Historians and geographers have long since moved beyond
the environmental determinism that characterized early writing
on the relationships between European settlers and nature.

Early farmers, however, didn't have the luxury of academic debates about what motivated their land use practices. The patterns of forest clearing for agriculture, followed by abandonment and reforestation, clearly reflect topography and the quality of the original soils and then the availability of good, cheap land to the west. The earliest European farmers settled the few natural meadows along the coast and in the lowlands and river valleys, fields left by former Native American communities or sites we would now recognize as seasonal wetlands and former beaver meadows. Subsequent waves of settlers had to move onto the far more challenging terrain of the hillslopes and uplands. The timing of forest clearing and early agricultural practices varied enormously from place to place, making it hard to sketch much more than general outlines of the agricultural history of the region as a whole. Luckily, the rich American tradition of town historians means that almost anyone in the Northeast has access to a wealth of local history.

I have lived in the Hudson Valley of New York for most of my life, and it is that history I know best. The portion of Dutchess County where I live was purchased by nine New York City businessmen (the Nine Partners) from the English Crown in 1697. The tract of fifty-nine thousand hectares included over six kilometers of some of the last good, undeveloped frontage on the east side of the Hudson River between New York City and Albany and stretched from the reasonably well-settled banks of the Hudson east through undeveloped wilderness to the Connecticut border. It seems fair to describe the Nine Partners as land speculators. During the first few decades after they purchased it their primary source of income from the land appears to have been from trapping beaver for the hat trade in England. But under pressure from the Crown to open up land for new settlers, the partners had most of the tract surveyed by

1740, and settlers began purchasing acreage of largely unbroken forest and moving into the interior of the county. There would have been very little in the way of natural openings and no large river floodplains to clear, so most of the agriculture required clearing forests from thin, rocky upland soils. The region quickly developed a thriving wheat crop that represented a farmer's primary source of income and an important source of wheat for the new republic. Yields of that cash crop just as quickly faded as a result of the inherently poor quality of the soils and the arrival of an insect pest, the Hessian fly, and a pathogen, wheat rust, both of which were inadvertently introduced from the Old World. The Hessian fly was considered enough of a strategic threat to the country's wheat supply that Thomas Jefferson was appointed chair of a new committee of the American Philosophical Society charged with finding means to combat it. In 1791 he and James Madison took a trip through New England and upstate New York during which he visited with farmers and took notes on the impacts of the fly.[1]

The opening of the Erie Canal in 1825 was an important turning point in the ecological history of the Hudson Valley. As wheat yields and soil fertility declined there, the opening of rich soils in the Ohio Valley proved irresistible to many farmers in Dutchess County. More critically, the canal meant they could send produce back east to Albany, from thence to New York City and onward to Europe. The population of Clinton, the town where I live, peaked in the 1820 census and did not exceed that level until 1950. As farmers emigrated to the Midwest, those who stayed behind could purchase their neighbor's land and keep just the best fields in production. And while the numbers of farmers declined, the sizes of farms and diversity of farming practices expanded dramatically during the century between the opening of the Erie Canal and the Great Depression. By 1915 an agricul-

tural extension publication for Dutchess County noted that over
80 percent of the land in the county had been "improved," that
is, cleared of forests. But even farmers needed forests, so woodlots persisted in wet areas and on marginal soils and steep slopes
as a source of timber and firewood. Thus the remnant original
forests in the region were almost all subjected to frequent logging
and occurred only on the poorest soils and steepest slopes.

The Great Depression of the 1930s, the next important
pivot in the ecological history of the region, marked the real
beginning of the rebound in northeastern forest cover as farms
failed and were abandoned. The early stages of that rebound
are marked by highly diverse ecological communities dominated by shrubs and herbaceous species that have essentially
no analogue in the pre-European landscape. Ecologists refer to
these communities with the prosaic but apt term "old fields."
They have been a ubiquitous feature of the eastern landscape
for the past century, but are gradually disappearing as trees
invade and shade out the shrubs and herbs (fig. 9). A number
of years ago Peter Marks of Cornell University asked what in
retrospect seems the most salient question: if old fields were a
cultural artifact of recent abandonment of farm fields, where
were all those old-field species hanging out in the twelve thousand years before such widespread agriculture? The answer for
a significant fraction of the old-field flora is that they were
European natives themselves and were brought to the New
World either inadvertently or deliberately by the colonists. But
the native old-field species, particularly species like the goldenrods and little bluestem grasses, were likely very rare prior
to European settlement and restricted to marginal sites like
ridgetops and stream banks kept open by stressful conditions
or frequent disturbance. The open vegetation afforded by these
old-field plants provided habitat for a number of species of

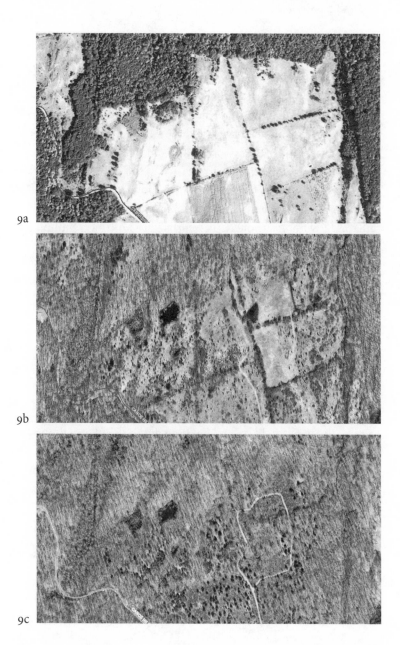

9a

9b

9c

insects, birds, and mammals that were equally likely to have been rare prior to European settlement but that flourished in the ideal conditions present in abandoned farm fields.[2]

There are two very different ecological legacies of these patterns of intensive agriculture followed by abandonment. The first concerns the fate of the native forest understory of shrubs and herbaceous species. Most of them are shade tolerant and are rarely found in the old-field communities that colonize abandoned farmland. Perhaps unexpectedly, trees are the first of the native forest plants to reestablish. Their shade will eventually drive out the shade-intolerant old-field species, creating a diversity bottleneck with a canopy of a few tree species but a relatively empty understory. Many of the native understory species have limited means of seed dispersal, but that alone doesn't seem sufficient to explain their slow rates of reestablish-

---

Figures 9a–c. Aerial photos showing the reforestation via old-field succession of a set of abandoned agricultural fields at The Cary Institute in 1942 (*a*), 1980 (*b*), and 2016 (*c*). The fields were pastures for a dairy farm owned by John Henry and were abandoned from use by 1932, soon after purchase of the land by Mary Flagler Cary. The swales and wetter portions of the fields in 1942 were dominated by goldenrods (several species in the genus *Solidago*), the native shrub gray dogwood (*Cornus racemosa*), and nonnative honeysuckles (*Lonicera morrowi*). The thinner soils of the hilltops were dominated by grasses, primarily little bluestem grass (*Schizachyrium scoparium*). In 1980 the site was still dominated by grasses and shrubs. The first trees to colonize these fields were eastern red cedars (*Juniperus virginiana*, distinguishable as the dark dots in the fields). Over time, gray dogwood also spread into the grass-dominated portions of the fields, and hardwood trees began to colonize. By 2016 the fields were rapidly transitioning to a closed forest canopy, with few remnants of the old-field grasses and shrubs. Photo credit: Aerial Access, Dutchess County, NY, https://gis.dutchessny.gov/aerialaccess.

ment in the resurrected forests. Postagricultural forests with eighty-year-old trees in the woods at the Cary Institute still have a distinctively different understory than the few woodlots on hillslopes that were never put into cultivation or were used for pasture. One of the best botanical clues to land use history in the Cary Institute woods is the presence of the shrub maple-leaved viburnum (*Viburnum acerifolium*). It is the most common native shrub in former woodlots and will occur right up to the stone wall that separates the woodlot from an adjacent postagricultural forest but will rarely be found on the other side of the wall. Over the years I've entertained a number of ideas to explain this but frankly don't have a good explanation for the shrub's slow rate of spread. My favorite hypothesis blames deer and small mammals that graze in the forest understory. That hypothesis presumes that the grazing can prevent establishment of new populations but can be tolerated by well-established populations on the woodlot side of the stone wall. Some studies suggest it could take centuries for a representative community of native understory plants to reestablish.[3]

Unlike the records of tree pollen deposited in lake sediments and witness trees recorded by land surveyors, our best information on the presettlement distribution and abundance of native shrubs and herbs comes from the field notes and writings of a small number of early botanical explorers. There are so few old-growth forests left on soils that were suited to agriculture that we can't rely on those rare preserves as our baseline. So while trees have become reestablished on an astonishing fraction of the southern New England landscape, I have little hope that I will ever get to witness the botanical richness that those sites once possessed and am not sure I even have a clear picture of just how glorious that community might have been.[4]

The second legacy traces back to whether a field was in cultivation or was used as pasture just before abandonment. Oaks appear to have been the overwhelmingly dominant species in presettlement forests of the Hudson Valley, representing 80 percent of the witness trees, for example, in the original deeds from the Nine Partners for the roughly eight hundred hectares that became the Cary Institute property. And it appears to have been common practice one hundred years ago to leave scattered oaks in fields used as pasture. The pastures were often found on the least fertile, most drought-prone fields. The old-field communities that form on abandoned pastures are often dominated by the grass little bluestem, which I consider the most beautiful of our native grasses, although with the inelegant scientific name of *Schizachyrium scoparium*. But presumably because of the local seed source provided by those scattered trees, oaks are a significant component of the forest canopy that eventually develops on those grasslands. The energy reserves in their large acorns may have been critical in allowing the new seedlings to quickly build enough of a root system to survive the summer droughts that often occur on those soils. In contrast, oaks are far less common as the initial woody colonists of fields abandoned from cultivation. While both squirrels and some birds will actively disperse acorns, the vast majority of acorns will land within a few meters of the parent oak tree. In contrast, species like red maple, white pine, and white ash are the most common woody invaders on our fields abandoned from culti- vation. Their wind-dispersed seeds are large enough to help the seedlings get established in competition with the old-field shrubs and herbs, particularly on less stressful sites, but they are small enough that their modest wings allow them to disperse well out from the hedgerows and adjacent forests. While it seems clear that oaks were the original occupants of those abandoned cultivated fields, there is little reason to believe the oaks will ever reclaim their former dominance there.

This cycle of forest clearing, intensive agriculture, abandonment, and forest regrowth played out throughout the lower elevations of the northeastern United States and indeed up and down the eastern seaboard. The steeper slopes and higher elevations of the highlands and mountains of the Northeast had a very different fate. There, logging was the prime agent of disturbance to presettlement forests. The visual ravages of that early logging are often cited as one of the catalysts for the nascent environmental awareness of the late nineteenth century. Clearing land for agriculture was considered to improve the land. But clear-cutting a forest for timber or to strip the bark from the hemlocks for the tanning industry was a messy business and without question was justifiably seen as a threat to rivers and streams. I've always wondered what the now-famous trout streams of the Catskills must have been like when that region was dotted with massive tanneries in the 1830s that were stripping the hillsides of hemlocks and dumping tanning effluent into every watershed.[5] Farther north, before the railroads were built, water was the primary mode of transport for logs. The deliberate damming of rivers upstream so that they could be filled with logs over the winter and then dynamited in the spring to flush the logs down to the mills must have been an awe-inspiring spectacle and extraordinarily dangerous work.

But, somewhat paradoxically, I would argue that despite the public outcry at the time, early logging practices did not set our forests off on fundamentally new courses, at least in comparison to the lasting impact of agriculture. Just as the details of agricultural history varied according to local environments, cultures, and economies, there are many diverse local narratives about early logging in the Northeast. Conifers were the most prized targets for early loggers, whether it was white pine on the Maine coast, hemlock in the Catskills, or red and white spruce along river valleys of the Adirondacks. It was certainly an ignominious fate for a three-hundred-year-old hemlock to be felled simply to be stripped of its bark for the tanneries while the trunk was left to rot where it fell. But turnover is a constant feature of the forest canopy. Once railroads were available to carry hardwood logs that wouldn't float down the rivers, the era of intensive northern logging began in earnest. Regardless of what species was being harvested, there are only minor differences in the ecological consequences of being cut down versus uprooted or snapped off by a windstorm or dying while standing in place from natural causes. Much of the earliest logging in northern forests occurred in winter, when snow cushioned the ground from soil disturbance. Unlike the effects of plowing, soil erosion, and ultimately soil rebuilding from two hundred years of farming, early logging had only minor impacts on forest soils. And unlike the elimination of the forest understory by agriculture, early logging would have had little lasting impact on native understory species. It is certainly true that logging triggered successional dynamics that are still playing out, and there is no question that many early successional and less shade-tolerant tree species are more common today than in the presettlement forests because of logging disturbance.[6] But the changes triggered by that early logging are quantitative—higher abundance of early successional trees and young forests—rather than fundamentally new successional pathways.

5

Seared into Memory
Legacies of Fire and Fire Suppression

Spring is fire season in eastern forests, and each year it is the beginning of the ever-worsening calamity that has become the fire season in western forests. Both regions experienced massive conflagrations over a century ago, with consequences that still shape public perception and policies. The Big Burn of 1910 torched 1.2 million hectares of northern Idaho and adjacent parts of Washington and Montana.[1] The same period saw two massive fire seasons in the northern Adirondacks: fires in 1903 burned over 200,000 hectares and destroyed several small towns, and even greater acreage burned in 1908. The severity of the Adirondack fires resulted from a potent combination of factors, including unusually dry spring and summer conditions, which combined with ample fuel from the slash left by widespread logging and abundant sources of ignition from sparks thrown by locomotives on new railroads built for that wave of clear-cutting.

All across the country foresters responded with remarkably effective policies to suppress fires before they could spread. Today, abandoned fire towers dotting hilltops are perhaps the most visible symbol of those early years of fire suppression. But the response to those early disasters has had long-term legacies that are in many ways just as disastrous, both in human terms and in less tragic but still pervasive ecological terms. In western forests decades of fire suppression sowed the seeds for the ultimate and ultimately catastrophic failure of the policy as fuel accumulated, leading in many forests to uncontrollable fires far more severe than would have burned naturally. In the East a very different dynamic has played out. Fire suppression has created forests and landscapes that appear to be less prone to the spread of even light ground fires, let alone the massive crown fires of one hundred years ago that live on in the institutional memories of state and local foresters. And in many forests in the Northeast, particularly those that were historically dominated by oaks, fire suppression is believed by many ecologists to have initiated an inexorable replacement of the fire-tolerant oaks by more fire-sensitive species like maples.

It's hard not to see early twentieth-century fire management as part and parcel of the can-do American spirit of wresting control of nature and its resources. In ecological terms suppressing fires fit neatly within a view of nature in which any disturbance interrupted the desired climax forests. But by the middle of the century ecologists across the country were realizing just how integral fire was to the functioning of many ecosystems. As is often the case, it took years of meticulous fieldwork for those ideas to take hold. Some of the best early work was done in northern Minnesota in the pine, spruce, and birch forests of the prairie-forest border. Foresters in the 1950s documented widespread evidence of the fire origins of many stands. And while those fires were what we would now call stand-replacing—intense fires that killed most trees and triggered a new wave of succession—the fires were patchy enough that some trees survived. And, more critically, many of the surviving trees had scars at the base of the trunk, formed where some portion of the base was subjected to sufficient heat that it killed the inner bark. The resulting wound would be gradually closed by growth of the surrounding wood and bark. By cutting a wedge out of the trunk through the old wound ecologists could date the previous fire by counting back through the tree rings produced since the scar was formed. On some trees they could date not just one but several successive fires.

Miron Heinselman spent years in the 1960s and 1970s in a canoe crisscrossing the remaining unlogged forests of the Boundary Waters region of northern Minnesota, dating fire scars and producing detailed maps of the distribution of stands that dated from individual fires.[2] He concluded that in presettlement times there was a significant fire somewhere in the region on average every four years. To my mind the lasting scientific legacy of his work was not that fires were frequent in the presettlement forests of the Boundary Waters but rather the shift in focus his work demanded: from the dynamics of disturbance and recovery of an individual stand to the dynamics of the mosaic of stands at different successional stages within the broader, fire-dependent landscape.

Heinselman's approach to reconstructing the presettlement fire regime of the Boundary Waters has been the foundation of an enormous body of research in the past fifty years that documents the natural fire regimes of the conifer forests of the western United States and boreal forests across Canada. Ecologists in the East have faced a more difficult challenge. As I noted in chapter 3, both the pollen record and presettlement witness trees suggest that catastrophic fires were infrequent in presettlement forests of the northeastern United States, except on the sandiest and thinnest soils (fig. 10).[3] There is abundant

Figure 10. A pitch pine barrens on bedrock along the Shawangunk Ridge in southeastern New York. The pitch pines at this site typically reach only five to ten meters in height, with an open canopy and an abundant layer of native ericaceous shrubs, including mountain laurel, huckleberries, and several species of blueberries. In the absence of fire, this site will gradually be invaded by taller tree species such as white pine and red maple. Photo by author.

evidence, both physical and written, that forest fires were common in the eighteenth and nineteenth centuries as a result of the activities of European settlers. But frequent low-intensity fires that are assumed to have slowly spread through the understory of a presettlement oak forest, killing only scattered trees, leave little lasting physical evidence. This is even more true of the large fraction of current oak forests of southern New England that went through the gauntlet of repeated logging of the remnant woodlots on hillslopes or reestablishment on abandoned pastures. The presence of charcoal in lake sediments remains the primary physical evidence for presettlement fire in the Northeast but translating that record into anything resembling a detailed reconstruction of a regional fire regime has proven elusive.

Despite the difficulties of reconstructing the kind of detailed fire histories that western ecologists have access to, twenty years ago I would have had little hesitation in accepting that frequent low-intensity fires were critical to the existence of eastern oak forests, at least as they were found at the time of European settlement. The disturbing corollary is that fire suppression might spell the demise of those forests or at least their transformation into very different forest ecosystems. While the evidence was indirect, it seemed compelling. The writings of the earliest European explorers contain frequent references to fire, at least along coastal regions of the Northeast, with the assumption that fires were often deliberately set by Native Americans. Those writings are anecdotal, however, and some ecologists have argued that deliberately set fires were at most a local occurrence around major Native American settlements. Emily Russell Southgate reviewed thirty-five firsthand descriptions of the presettlement landscape from the Carolinas to Maine that met her standards for historical credibility and noted that in not a single one of them did the author actually observe Native Americans setting fire to forests.[4] But fires require a source of ignition, and it is widely assumed that lightning-caused fires are relatively rare in eastern forests. Thus belief that fire was common in oak forests required invoking humans as the main source of ignition.

Oddly enough a lot of the debate over the role of fire in oak forests revolves around maples rather than oaks. Both red maple and sugar maple have increased dramatically in abundance in eastern forests over the past century, so much so that they are now the two most abundant tree species in the eastern United States.[5] And while sugar maple was common in witness tree records from more northern forests, neither species was particularly common in more southern forests of the Northeast, where oaks were predominant. Oaks made up roughly 80 percent of the witness trees in the presettlement forests of the Cary Institute in the Hudson Valley of New York, with only a few records of maple trees. Oaks are only half as abundant in the modern forests at the institute, and the two maples now make up roughly 40 percent of the canopy trees. The shift is even more pronounced if you look at the understory. None of the four common oak species in the institute woods are shade tolerant, and the more shade-tolerant maples vastly outnumber oaks in the seedling and sapling layers.

But while oaks are not particularly tolerant of shade, they are known to be much more tolerant of fire, at least in comparison with the maples. And not only are they more tolerant of fire than maples, but also their leaf litter is a more important source of fuel for surface fires in the spring. Oak leaves decompose much more slowly than maple leaves. So while maple leaves have largely decomposed and become compressed into the forest floor over winter, oak leaves still have much of their mass the next spring and are still stiff enough to avoid compression. As a result, a layer of oak leaves on a warm spring day is a perfect recipe for a ground fire, assuming there is a source of ignition. This difference in the flammability of oak versus maple leaf litter is at the heart of the potential for what ecologists think of as a regime shift. As maples gradually displace oaks, for whatever reasons, the likelihood of the spread of a fire decreases. This creates the opportunity for a positive feedback loop favoring even greater dominance by maples and other fire-intolerant species rather than oaks.

A shift from oak to maple dominance is a fundamental transformation of a forest ecosystem. Acorns are a far more valuable food resource than maple seeds for all manner of wildlife. The accelerated rate of decay of maple leaves creates an entirely different forest floor habitat for vertebrates and invertebrates that live there, along with faster rates of nutrient cycling through the soil and potential for leaching of nitrogen from the soil. And while the timber value of both sugar and red maple has increased in recent years, oaks still retain important economic value. All of these developments have fueled efforts by a dedicated community of forest managers, wildlife biologists, and ecologists to preserve eastern oak forests. Reintroducing controlled burns has been a key part of those efforts but with mixed results at best. Dozens of experiments using one or more controlled burns at different times of the year have been conducted in the past thirty years in oak forests from Alabama to New York (fig. 11). A recent review of those studies concluded that the effects on oak regeneration in mature forests were evenly split between positive, negative, and ambiguous.[6] In addition, the difficulties forest managers would face in reintroducing controlled burns in most oak forests, given concerns about threat to human life and property, are tremendous.

Figure 11. A controlled burn conducted as part of research on maintaining oak forests in the Hudson Valley of New York. Photo credit: John Mizel. Courtesy of the Mohonk Preserve.

My sense is that the uncertainty about the effectiveness of reintroducing fire has led to a crisis of confidence among both scientists and forest managers and that the debate about the role of fire in eastern oak forests has devolved into three highly dissimilar questions with different implications for the future of those forests. The first is in the province of anthropologists and paleoecologists: how important was fire as a mechanism that led to oak dominance in many presettlement forests of eastern North America? Just as critical would be understanding what types of fires were responsible, that is, what time of the year did they burn, how frequently, and with what severity? The exact source of ignition would be a peripheral question, and I would leave it to the anthropologists to assess whether Native Americans were in fact the prime agent. The challenge has come from some paleoecologists who question the strength of evidence for the historical importance of fire in presettlement oak forests and propose that episodic severe droughts offer an alternative explanation.[7] In their analysis the rise of maples in the past century coincides with a period with fewer severe droughts. An obvious rejoinder would be that there is ample evidence that fire years coincide with drought years, so it's not easy to disentangle the two. The paleoecological evidence for the role of drought is correlative, just like the evidence for the role of fire from the charcoal found in lake sediments. But the actual mechanism by which infrequent but severe droughts actually maintain oak dominance and inhibit almost all maples is not at all clear to me. Given what we know about variation in the drought tolerance of different life history stages of the maples and oaks, I find it much easier to see a causal pathway for oak dominance as a result of periodic fire than because of periodic droughts alone. But I have concluded that we are unlikely to ever truly resolve the debate about the importance of fire in presettlement oak forests, let alone with any precision about the critical details of the seasonal timing, frequency, or severity of those fires. The historical record and physical evidence are simply too sparse.

The second and perhaps more pertinent question is, then, how important has fire suppression been in the decline in oak dominance and the rise of maples over the past century? There is no question that fire suppression has been extremely successful in most places. Spring fires on the rocky, oak-dominated hilltops of the Hudson Highlands, for instance, stubbornly resist suppression and are capable of spreading even below-ground. But fire has been absent from the vast majority of oak forests for most of the past century, and there is no question that maples have increased dramatically in abundance during that same period. The notion that oaks are fire tolerant and maples intolerant is well established in the scientific literature and provides at least a plausible mechanism for a link between fire suppression and increased maple abundance.

But many of the current oak forests owe their existence to traits other than just their fire tolerance. Oak forests that were never cleared for agriculture were spared in most cases because their soils were too rocky or steep. But even on those sites they were heavily and repeatedly logged for timber, firewood, charcoal production, and tanbark. All of our common oak species sprout copiously from a cut stump, and the sprouts can put on impressive height growth in full sun. They also benefited from the scarcity of their nemesis, the white-tailed deer, which had been hunted so heavily that they had to be reintroduced to southern New England in the early 1900s. And the current abundance of red maple is not due only to its ability to invade oak forests in the absence of fire. As I described in chapter 3, many of the oak forests that were cleared for agriculture and then abandoned from cultivation (rather than from pasture) were successfully colonized by light-seeded, wind-dispersed species like the maples, birches, and ashes rather than by oaks with their large acorns. Moreover, like the oaks, red maple sprouts prolifically from a cut stump and can put on height growth in full sun nearly as rapidly as red oak. Many of the field experiments testing the effects of fire on oak regeneration conclude that oak seedlings and saplings are in fact vulnerable to fire and suggest that they may need several decades or more of a fire-free period to get safely established before their thick bark can protect them. So there are currents other than fire suppression that have worked both for and against the oaks over the past century. But like the question of the importance of fire in presettlement forests, the role of fire suppression in the displacement of oaks by maples over the past century is still a matter of history, with all of the attendant uncertainty inherent in ascribing exact causes to past events.

This leads to the third and perhaps most salient question for anyone who values oak forests: what if anything can and should be done to reverse the decline in oak abundance in eastern forests? Is it really necessary to reintroduce fire in order to save them, or are there other interventions and forces that will promote oaks? I would like to think that there are large enough oak forest preserves in at least some portions of their historic range where scientists and land managers can perfect fire management as a tool to restore oak dominance. There is a risk that these sites would simply become living museums, and expensive ones at that, since controlled burns are risky enough that managers and nearby residents demand large fire crews standing by. But given the financial and political limitations I see little chance that active fire management can reverse the broad regional decline in oak abundance. The obvious alternative is to turn to active forest management and logging regimes that favor oak regeneration. In most parts of the Northeast this approach would require a deliberate program to reduce deer densities since acorns and oak seedlings and saplings are a favorite food for white-tailed deer in the fall and winter. Unfortunately, social and economic forces in southern New England have combined to do just the opposite, as hunters lobby for more deer and landowners favor highly selective logging that often targets just the large oak trees but without creating openings large enough to give adequate light levels for vigorous oak regeneration. Thus while the tools exist to allow a determined landowner to reverse the decline in his or her own woods, it would take a sea change in public attitudes to reverse the broader tide.

6

The Fall and Rise of the White-Tailed Deer

The extraordinary decline and rebound of eastern forests over the past two centuries is mirrored in the fates of many of the animals that inhabited those forests. Some, like the woodland bison and eastern elk, were likely very rare in the heavily forested Northeast, but even along the midwestern prairie–forest border these grassland and woodland species were extirpated by the mid-1800s, and elk have only recently been reintroduced to eastern forests.[1] The iconic large predators of eastern forests, the wolf and the cougar, were largely eliminated from the Northeast by the late 1800s and extirpated by the early twentieth century. And while there are groups that have advocated the reintroduction of these keystone predators, state wildlife agencies have no appetite for the political battles that would ensue. But the abundance of the white-tailed deer (*Odocoileus virginianus*), one of the most common large mammals in eastern forests and the primary prey of wolves and cougars, tracks almost perfectly the dramatic decline in forest cover during the late nineteenth and early twentieth centuries and the equally impressive rebound during the past one hundred years. If you're a deer hunter or a state wildlife biologist, the recovery of eastern white-tailed deer is a remarkable success story. But if you're a forester or a forest ecologist or a gardener (or a driver, for that matter), the recovery is decidedly a mixed blessing.

While the dramatic fluctuations in forest cover and abundance of deer over the past two centuries are similar in timing and magnitude, there is no direct causal connection between the two patterns. Forests recovered in large part on their own, following abandonment of agricultural land and reductions in rates of clear-cutting. The recovery of white-tailed deer required strict laws regulating hunting and intensive wildlife management at the state level, with support from the well-organized, politically powerful community of deer hunters. There are no hard estimates of the abundance of white-tailed deer in the Northeast prior to European settlement, but various authors suggest that densities would have been roughly four deer per square kilometer in the eastern United States. There is every reason to believe that numbers of deer varied widely across the region and over time due to differences in Native American hunting pressure, habitat quality, and winter severity. The European settlement that brought so much forest clearing also brought very high hunting pressure, and by the mid-nineteenth century deer were already scarce across southern New England. The Forest Commission of New York concluded in 1887 that "it is fair to suppose that there are not a dozen deer in [the] whole Catskill region." By the late 1800s most of the surviving deer in New York were found in refugia in the Adirondack Mountains. Deer are assumed to have been effectively extirpated from the entire state of Connecticut by the end of the 1800s.[2]

In response, states began passing laws limiting or even banning deer hunting outright. In many parts of New York, particularly the southern and western portions of the state, deer hunting was effectively banned during most of the years between the turn of the twentieth century and the beginning of World War II. By any standard those laws, combined with hunter education that focused on harvesting bucks but not the does, have been wildly successful over the past seventy-five years. The population of a dozen or so deer in the Catskills has rebounded to the point that 6,680 deer were legally killed during the 2017 hunting season in the five wildlife management units that comprise the Catskill region. Even if the 2017 Catskill harvest took as much as half of the current population, there are a thousand times more deer in the region than there were at their nadir in 1887.

Reliable estimates of the modern abundance of white-tailed deer are almost as hard to come by as estimates for pre-settlement times. The time-honored method is to go out in the spring and walk transects through the woods, counting the number of piles of deer droppings, or pellet groups, that have accumulated on top of the previous fall's leaf litter. The calculation requires a guesstimate of the average number of pellet groups produced by a single deer each day over winter. One commonly used figure is an astonishing twenty-five per deer per day. This gives you an idea of how much browsing deer need to do each day and how low the quality of the nutrition in their winter diet. A more modern and expensive method uses aerial surveys in the winter from aircraft equipped with forward-looking infrared cameras. Neither method is used extensively enough that it has produced a map of deer density in a reasonably sized landscape that I trusted. Regardless of method, it is widely assumed that deer densities in the heavily forested regions of the Northeast are at least twice as high (eight to sixteen per square kilometer) as in presettlement times and as much as ten to fifteen times higher (greater than sixty deer per square kilometer) in the more fragmented southern portions of the region, where deer have access to cropland and suburban landscaping.[3]

Although it is difficult to accurately estimate deer population density, the effects of the current high numbers of deer are easy to document. The standard technique is to simply erect small fenced areas in the understory of a forest and compare tree regeneration within those exclosures to nearby unfenced areas. These experiments have been conducted many times throughout the Northeast, and the results are depressingly consistent. Within a few years the area inside the fence will be dense with seedlings and small saplings of trees, while outside the fence few seedlings are more than knee high and there are few saplings at all. The exceptions are in areas with deliberate hunting programs focused on shooting does and reducing the number of deer well below regional averages or in the far north, where severe winters limit the abundance of deer. The problem is readily apparent in forest inventory data (fig. 12). There are no hard-and-fast thresholds for the numbers of seedlings and saplings that should be present in a healthy forest, but the maps in figure 12 illustrate variation in the densities of seedlings and saplings in the more than thirty-three thousand forest inventory plots routinely sampled by the US Forest Service in the nine northeastern states. The highest classes are levels that our modeling suggests are high enough to indicate there is no significant reduction in overall forest biomass and productivity due to poor regeneration. Fewer than 4 percent of the plots have seedling densities that high, and fewer than 8 percent of the plots have that many saplings. Most of these plots are found in

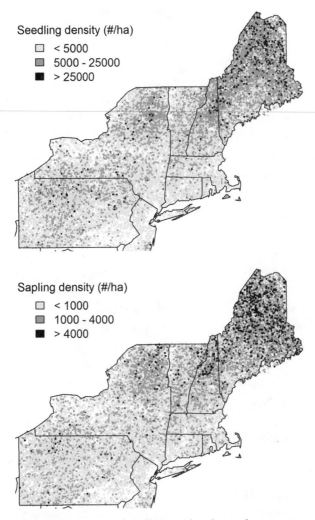

Figure 12. Densities of seedlings and saplings of tree species in censuses of 33,310 forest inventory plots in the nine northeastern states. Seedlings are defined as individuals with stems less than 2.54 centimeters in diameter and taller than 15 centimeters for conifers and 30 centimeters for hardwood species. Saplings are individuals greater than 2.54 centimeters in stem diameter and less than 12.7 centimeters in stem diameter.

the far north, where winters are severe, the landscape is heavily forested, and deer densities are presumably the lowest. In contrast, 55 percent of northeastern forests have seedling and sapling densities in the lowest class. At these levels there is no question that forest biomass and productivity are significantly reduced and that composition can be tilted to tree species that are not browsed as heavily. The basis for the reduction is simple: eventually some saplings, particularly saplings of less palatable species, will get tall enough to escape browsing by the deer. But it takes much longer for those saplings to replace a canopy tree that dies, and the new canopy has a much lower density of new, small trees.

It is harder to generalize about the effects of overabundant white-tailed deer on forest composition. There is no question that individual deer can be highly selective of which species of seedlings and saplings they browse. The challenge is that the choices of what to browse can vary greatly from place to place, in part because of variation in the food choices locally available to the deer. For example, in northern forests containing a mix of hardwoods and conifers, spruce and balsam fir saplings will only be lightly browsed, as the deer focus on the hardwoods and more palatable conifers like hemlock and yew. It is almost certainly not a coincidence that almost 20 percent of the saplings in forests in Vermont and New Hampshire are the more lightly browsed balsam fir and red spruce, while those two species make up only about 10 percent of the biomass of canopy trees. But on conifer-dominated Anticosti Island in the St. Lawrence River introduction of deer and maintenance of high deer densities for the benefit of hunters has largely eradicated balsam fir, with little impact on the native spruces.[4]

One of my favorite studies on deer browsing patterns was done in Black Rock Forest in the Hudson Highlands in the

1930s. Researchers there were doing some of the first experiments to test whether northeastern forests would respond to fertilization and noticed that deer focused their browsing in plots that had been fertilized with nitrogen. Many tree species will take up nitrogen in excess of their immediate needs for growth—a process known as luxury consumption—and store the extra nitrogen in their roots and shoots in the form of amino acids. This translates into higher protein content in the woody material consumed by deer. Chris Tripler and colleagues and I repeated this experiment in the late 1990s at Great Mountain Forest. Browse frequency was consistently higher on saplings that had been fertilized, but the differences were statistically significant for only six of the nine tree species in the experiment that consumed nitrogen in excess of demand. In that experiment fertilized saplings were located several meters away from paired unfertilized saplings of the same species. Given that choice, deer would typically browse the fertilized sapling heavily, while often leaving the unfertilized sapling untouched. I learned to respect greatly the sophistication of deer foraging from Tripler's work.[5]

The effects of overabundant deer are not limited to inhibiting tree regeneration. Researchers typically document large differences in the shrubs and herbaceous species present inside versus outside exclosures. Foresters for obvious reasons focus their concerns on patterns of winter browsing on woody stems, typically the only material available for the deer to eat at that time of year. But deer are fundamentally grazers, not browsers, and obtain most of their annual nutrition from grazing on herbaceous plants, not woody ones. It is common to observe that areas inside deer exclosures have vastly higher abundance of broadleaf herbs, while the surrounding areas subject to grazing by deer have greater cover of less palatable grasses, sedges, and ferns and lower plant diversity overall. Studies have also documented much lower rates of invasion by nonnative plants like garlic mustard (*Alliaria petiolata*) and stiltgrass (*Microstegium vimineum*) when deer are excluded. Reductions in the abundance of native shrubs due to deer can have cascading effects on other animals, particularly species of small mammals like the white-footed mouse and of birds like the eastern wood pewee that use shrub layers for nesting and habitat.[6]

There is mounting evidence that the impacts of deer on the understory community of shrubs and herbaceous species can create a feedback loop that makes tree regeneration even more problematic. The white-tailed deer in the accompanying photograph (fig. 13) is standing in a dense thicket of hayscented fern (*Dennstaedtia punctilobula*), likely with scattered New York fern (*Thelypteris noveboracensis*). Hayscented fern is native, and while it does not require high deer densities to establish such dense thickets exclosure studies have shown much lower fern abundance in areas where deer are excluded. Even in the absence of any effects of deer, dense thickets of hayscented fern can have measurable impacts on seedling recruitment and growth. Light levels at the ground beneath the ferns are typically as low as beneath a dense canopy of shade-tolerant species. This can effectively eliminate recruitment of all but the most shade-tolerant tree seedlings. The ferns also provide habitat for small mammals, particularly white-footed mice (*Peromyscus leucopus*) and red-backed voles (*Myodes gapperi*), that are voracious consumers of tree seeds and seedlings, respectively. Of even greater concern, there is evidence that dense fern cover and its effects on tree regeneration can persist long after deer densities are reduced.[7]

You could fill library shelves with the scientific studies that assess the impacts of local deer densities by using fenced

Figure 13. A white-tailed deer among a dense layer of hayscented fern (*Dennstaedtia punctilobula*). Photo by author.

areas to exclude deer. Those studies compare the effects of the local, often unmeasured, density of deer at the time of the study to what you could expect if there were no deer present at all. This is a good illustration of both the scientific strengths and weaknesses of controlled experiments. The exclosure studies are a convincing way to test whether local the local abundance of deer, whatever it may be, is having an effect on whatever ecological attribute you are measuring. But the studies do so only in comparison to what would happen in the complete absence of deer, that is, inside the fenced areas. No one is advocating eliminating deer, and the critical question for forest managers and wildlife biologists is what deer density can balance the interests of both hunters and foresters. At this point the most we can say is that deer densities throughout most of

the northeastern United States are high enough to have significant negative effects on tree regeneration and forest productivity. We are a long way from knowing just how far those
levels would need to be reduced to mitigate those impacts, while
still providing the ecological functions of a sustainable population of deer and the economic benefits of recreational hunting.

The future abundance of white-tailed deer will be one of
the currents that shapes the future of eastern forests. But it is
far from clear what the future holds for deer. No other species
of wildlife in the Northeast is caught up in such politically
charged debates among so many groups with competing interests. I have a great deal of sympathy for the difficulty state
wildlife officials face in balancing these often diametrically
opposed interests. For many years deer management was the
province of wildlife biologists in state agencies, and deer hunters were their only constituents and also the source of much of
the funding for wildlife management and research through the
taxes and license fees they paid. Early hunting regulations had
the simple goals of increasing the population of deer and pre-
serving a high-quality, safe recreational opportunity for hunters.
This objective generally involved limiting the take of females
and concentrating hunters' effort on bucks. It is not uncommon
for the fall hunt in many states to kill more than 50 percent of
male deer alive at the start of the hunting season, a percentage
based on admittedly crude estimates of overall deer density
statewide. A harvest of this size had the predictable consequence
that there were few older and well-antlered male deer. But
because the hunting of females was prohibited, the population
of deer could continue to increase year after year. Today there
are probably as many sociologists as wildlife biologists studying
deer management, and "human dimensions" is the new buzz-
word in academic departments. Hunters are still the dominant

constituency, but farmers, foresters, and suburban landowners concerned about overabundance now routinely weigh in during the periodic ritual of setting statewide deer-hunting policies. When asked, hunters will agree that controlling deer density is necessary and that deer populations should be kept in balance with food supplies. And while foresters can point to irrefutable evidence that densities throughout most of the Northeast are too high for forest health—and for an adequate supply of browse to keep deer healthy through the winter—surveys of hunters consistently show that they believe deer densities are still too low.[8] One of the most consistent predictors of hunter satisfaction is simply the number of deer they observe while in the woods, regardless of the age, sex, or health of the animals they see. There is ample evidence that deer minimize their movements at the start of hunting season, thereby reducing their visibility to hunters. The average age of hunters is steadily increasing, and hunting methods increasingly rely on the use of deer stands at fixed locations. I've begun to wonder if hunters' recent worries about seeing fewer deer each year are simply due to smarter deer and older, less mobile hunters.

Given these attitudes within the hunting community, it's not a surprise that state hunting regulations have been largely unsuccessful at reducing deer densities to levels that allow healthy levels of tree regeneration. The oldest and most ingrained impediment is probably the reluctance of hunters to take does, even in states where permits for taking antlerless deer have become widely available. There are other constraints as well. For example, a significant proportion of the landscape in most states is off-limits to hunters, either because landowners don't allow hunting or because of regulations prohibiting hunting near the ever-growing number of rural and suburban homes and structures.

There are some bright spots, however. It has become clear
that at least in limited areas an intensive hunting program with
a community of hunters who accept the management goals can
reduce deer density to levels that produce both a healthy herd
and healthy forests. For over forty years the Cary Institute has
used a deliberate hunting program focused on removing adult
females to control deer density on its roughly eight-hundred-
hectare property in the Hudson Valley of New York.[9] Indices
of deer density have declined almost linearly over the past
thirty years, and exclosure studies on the property show that
current densities have no measurable impact on the forest
understory. The harvest of deer from the property has declined
from a high of over eighty to as few as twenty deer per year over
the same time period, and adult females comprise a third to
half of the total harvest in any given year. The volunteers who
hunt the property are active participants in the program and
have to agree to take a doe at least periodically to remain in the
program. In the early years of the program more than 75 percent
of the gun hunters would take one or more deer each year. That
number has dropped to around 50 percent in the past few years.
The hunters have been strong supporters of the program, however, and cite its safety, good but controlled access to the property, and low hunter numbers for their satisfaction.

The number of similar programs around the Northeast
appears to be growing. Some of the earliest studies that focused
on deer overabundance came from state and national parks that
allowed no hunting at all. Given the absence of their natural
predators, extraordinarily high deer densities in such locations
can virtually eliminate the forest understory. A number of parks
in the region are experimenting with introducing formal deer
hunts with deliberate emphasis on taking does. One of the
concerns with such programs is determining the minimum area

to be included in the controlled hunt, given the potentially large home ranges of white-tailed deer, particularly when they are present at high density and food is scarce. Luckily there has been a fair bit of research on deer movement patterns and territoriality, and it appears that deer are sedentary enough that a controlled hunt on an area of four hundred hectares or more can be sufficient for results not to be swamped by new deer moving in from surrounding areas.[10]

But those bright spots represent a small fraction of the forested landscape. And a recent wave of interest in promoting wildlife that use early successional habitat threatens to make the problem with deer overabundance even worse. During the middle of the last century, as forests began to recolonize abandoned farmland and as the wave of nineteenth- and early twentieth-century clear-cutting receded, young forests and old fields dominated by grasses and shrubs covered a large fraction of the northeastern landscape (see fig. 9). As a result of old-field succession and the transition from clear-cutting to selective logging in many forests, the fraction of the landscape in those kinds of habitats has inexorably declined. That fact is not in dispute. And there are many species of wildlife that make use of such habitats, although the number of species that truly depend on them is smaller. In the past decade a well-organized alliance of wildlife biologists, hunters, and foresters has formed with the goal of what is fundamentally an effort to re-create the northeastern landscape circa 1950, with the stated objective of promoting species of wildlife that use young forests and the grass- and shrub-dominated phases of old-field succession.[11]

White-tailed deer and a number of upland game birds are prominent on the list of species to be promoted, along with a number of species of songbirds, some reptiles, and a few species of small mammals like the New England cottontail. The primary tool the group advocates is basically a return to short-rotation clear-cutting. For example, New York State has adopted a plan to manage all state wildlife management units by clear-cutting 10 percent of the forests in each unit every ten years, under the assumption that "young forests" are defined as forests that were clear-cut within the past ten years. Unless some forests are set aside and allowed to mature, creating an even shorter rotation on the lands devoted to young forests, this state plan means that no forests on the units will be allowed to exceed one hundred years of age. There is a common assumption in forestry that northeastern forests are mature one hundred years after a clear-cut. I'm not entirely sure either where this misconception originated or just what constitutes maturity in this viewpoint. While forest productivity does gradually decline with stand age, forest inventory data suggest that aboveground biomass doesn't reach a steady state until well over two hundred years after a clear-cut. A forest landscape managed on a one-hundred-year rotation would be a far cry from any landscape that occurred prior to European settlement.

The websites advocating the return of young forests are full of pictures of songbirds, turtles, and other charismatic wildlife. Reading between the lines, though, it's not hard to see why both deer hunters and loggers support the initiative. There is no question that recent clear-cuts can provide more food for deer, particularly woody browse in the winter, compared to the decimation of the understories of a closed forest canopy by current deer densities. But foresters should be prepared to be disappointed by the regeneration they find in the clear-cuts. It is true that seedling and sapling density increases, on average, when the biomass of canopy trees is reduced by an intensive harvest. The fraction of forestland that has substandard densities of seedlings and saplings, however, actually increases in the most heavily logged stands, indicating that the majority of recent clear-cuts would be classified as having failure of tree regeneration. There are likely many reasons for this, but if you walk through a heavily cut stand in the Adirondacks you will find high rates of browsing by deer. While a forester would be dismayed by the poor regeneration, the concentration of deer activity in the recent clear-cut is a boon to a hunter looking for deer.

Given all of the various currents at work, I have little faith in anyone's ability to predict the future of deer densities in different parts of the Northeast. It is clear from the widely available forest inventory data and many field experiments that the current historically high abundance of deer is having a significant impact on tree regeneration, with cascading effects on forest structure, composition, and productivity. Hunters appear to remain convinced, however, that there aren't enough deer, and they continue to have a dominant voice within the councils that set state hunting policies. Outside of the hunting community, polls indicate that farmers and landowners would like to see fewer deer, but they have only limited tools at their disposal to make that happen. It's not uncommon for animal rights activists to protest the use by municipalities of professional hunters to reduce deer herds. There is some evidence that coyotes, a relatively recent arrival in the Northeast, are becoming more adept as predators of white-tailed deer, particularly fawns. Far more effective would be the reestablishment of populations of wolves and cougars, their major natural predators.[12] After hunting, automobiles are the second leading cause of deer deaths in most regions. But that could conceivably change. The ability to avoid impacts with deer might present the sternest test imaginable for the collision-avoidance systems being deployed in new cars. Less severe winters in a warming world can be expected to spread the pattern of poor tree regeneration (see fig. 12) into even the northernmost forests of the region. The responses of northeastern forests to climate change will be heavily dependent on the success of tree regeneration by both the current residents and species spreading northward. In fact, it seems certain that lower deer densities would lead to forests that were far more resilient in the face not just of climate change but also of air pollution and forest pests and pathogens. While the inexorable dynamics of reforestation and forest succession during the past century have created strong currents that will play out over at least the next century, the future of white-tailed deer and their future impacts on northeastern forests are far less certain.

7

A Sea Change in Logging

L ogging practices and pressures in the Northeast have varied enormously since the first wave of timber harvests after Europeans arrived. Many ecologists and foresters appear to think of the logging history of the region and indeed of the northern half of the country as a giant rolling wave of clear-cutting that washed westward across the continent, leaving a landscape of even-aged, maturing forests in its wake. This narrative may have been accurate fifty years ago. Today it ignores a sea change in harvest practices in northeastern forests and is being used to justify a resumption of clear-cutting in the Northeast for the ostensible benefit of wildlife.

Scientists tend to be very protective of their turf, and there has long been an uneasy truce between ecologists and foresters.[1] As a result, much of the ecological research on northeastern forests has been done in reserves that are not being logged. If logging is acknowledged, ecologists seem to assume that their job is to study the succession that happens after a disturbance like logging but leave the study of the details of harvest practices to the silviculturalists in forestry departments. A lot of my early research fit neatly into this mold. And it gave me an excuse to work in some of the region's most magnificent old-growth forests. Eventually I realized that working in managed forests afforded a more productive research setting because logging created a more diverse array of environments and successional stages to study. But I was still content to leave the details and implications of harvest practices to the silviculturalists.

This all changed ten years ago when a summer intern of mine, Nicole Rogers, wanted to do a project using long-term data from the network of forest inventory plots maintained throughout the country by the US Forest Service. I had been working with those data for a number of years, but I focused on ecological processes like tree competition and typically filtered out any stands that had been logged during the period of interest. Rogers's objectives required that we look at all plots, not just plots that hadn't been logged, and a stunning statistic jumped out at us. In forests in the nineteen states from Virginia and Kentucky north to Wisconsin and Maine, logging accounted for 58 percent of the mortality of adult trees. In other words, logging accounted for more mortality than all other causes, either natural or human-induced, combined. And of the demographic processes that govern tree population dynamics, mortality of adult trees is one of the most potent.[2]

My colleagues' and my analyses produced two other results that were just as astonishing to me. The first was that clear-cutting had been replaced by partial harvests as the dominant form of management in the Northeast, at least on an area basis (fig. 14). There was regional variation, with more clear-cutting in conifer forests of both the far north (Maine) and the south (Virginia). But very light selective logging that removes less than 20 percent of tree biomass is by far the most common harvest in the oak-dominated forests of southern portions of the region, consisting of Pennsylvania, New Jersey, southern New York, Massachusetts,

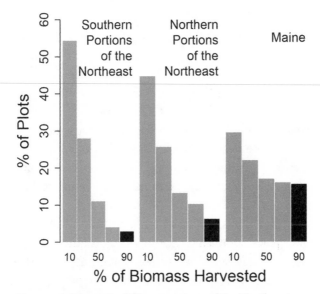

Figure 14. Forests in different regions of the Northeast are logged with very different intensities. The data come from US Forest Service Forest Inventory and Analysis plots sampled between 2003 and 2015 in upland forests in the nine northeastern states. Overall 2,307 of the 28,815 plots were logged during the typically five years between remeasurements at any given plot location.

Connecticut, and Rhode Island. Less than 3 percent of harvests on an area basis in that region are clear-cuts. Light selective logging still dominates in forests in northern parts of the region outside of Maine (consisting of northern New York and Vermont and New Hampshire), but intensive harvests—removing greater than 60 percent of biomass—made up over 16 percent of the stands that were logged. Maine has a distinctively different harvest regime, with almost a third of stands logged using intensive harvests that remove greater than 60 percent of tree biomass. But across the Northeast as a whole, the average harvest removed only roughly 30 percent of tree biomass. These partial harvests have been largely invisible to the public—that in fact could be one of the reasons for the shift away from clear-cutting. But it has also hidden a more disturbing consequence. For much of the past century one and a half to two times as much timber had been growing annually in the Northeast as was harvested. This re-flected both the steady increase in total forestland due to aban-donment of farmland and relatively modest levels of logging. The resulting carbon sequestration in northeastern forests has been an important offset to the nation's emissions of greenhouse gases.[3] Harvest levels, however, have been increasing steadily over the past fifty years, so much so that there seems little question that harvests in at least some states are now at unsustainable levels.

Maine is perhaps the most obvious example. Clear-cutting is still a common practice there, particularly in spruce/fir forests managed intensively for timber and fiber production. The concern is not over the ecological consequences of any single clear-cut, as those can be addressed when best management practices are followed. But the aggregate effects of so much clear-cutting are easily visible using Google Earth (figs. 15, 16). Recent clear-cuts and very young forests dominate large swaths of the state, particularly in the northern interior. As a result, average forest biomass per acre in Maine is only half that in the rest of the northeastern states, and average forest biomass has been declining in recent years. Its very young forests have lower productivity than older ones, and the state has the added misfortune of colder climates and less fertile soils.

Clear-cutting, however, isn't the only route to overharvest-ing. Connecticut is a prime example. Its oak forests are by any standard being high-graded, with only a small fraction of trees being harvested, typically the largest, most valuable individual

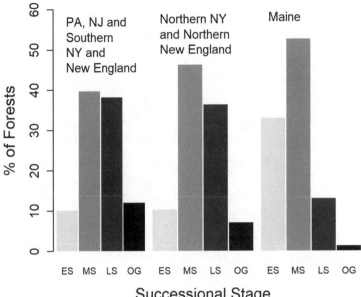

Figure 15a. The current distribution of northeastern forests in four broad successional stages, defined by aboveground tree biomass. Early successional forests (ES) are defined as stands with less than 50 metric tons per hectare of biomass. Mid-successional forests (MS) have between 50 and 150 metric tons per hectare. Late-successional forests (LS) have between 150 and 250 metric tons per hectare. Old-growth forests (OG) are defined as stands with greater than 250 metric tons per hectare. For reference, the average biomass of current upland forests in the nine state region is 129 metric tons per hectare, but ranges from 154 metric tons per hectare in the southern states to 141 metric tons per hectare in Vermont, New Hampshire, and the northern portion of New York, to eighty-five metric tons per hectare in Maine.

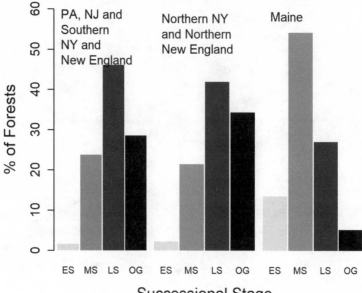

Figure 15b. The projected distribution of forests among the four successional stages in the year 2120, based on analyses by Michelle Brown, Charles D. Canham, Lora Murphy, and Therese M. Donovan, "Timber Harvest as the Predominant Disturbance Regime in Northeastern U.S. Forests: Effects of Harvest Intensification," *Ecosphere* 9 (2018): e02062. 10.1002/ecs2.2062. The projections assume maintenance of the current harvest regimes and include a projected climate change scenario. The characteristically light selective logging in states outside of Maine results in a significant increase in the proportion of the forested landscape in either late-successional or old-growth conditions. In Maine, by contrast, early and mid-successional forests continue to dominate. For reference, the average biomass of upland forests in the year 2120 is projected to increase to 166 metric tons per hectare, but ranges from 205 metric tons per hectare in the southern portion of the Northeast region to 216 metric tons per hectare in Vermont, New Hampshire, and the northern portion of New York to 125 metric tons per hectare in Maine.

Figure 16. An aerial image of a recent forest harvest in the Adirondack Mountains of New York. The harvested area in the right half of the image would probably be classified as a "variable retention" harvest—effectively a clear-cut with a small patch of conifers retained in the center and a few scattered residual trees. To the left is a comparably sized area of partial harvest with a much more substantial residual canopy. Photo by author.

trees (see fig. 14). Over the past decade harvests have been removing essentially all of the net growth, and average biomass in forests within the state has declined slightly in recent years.[4] The problem is exacerbated in Connecticut by suburban development that is slowly eating away at the forestland base.

These statistics are even worse when you dig deeper. The standard baseline for assessing the sustainability of harvests at a state or regional level has been to compare the balance of net growth of forest biomass (total tree growth minus natural tree mortality) and the removal of trees in harvests. If net growth exceeds removals over the entire land base, tree biomass will increase. The calculation of net growth and removals is typically done for all forestland in the region that is not legally restricted from logging. In reality, however, a significant fraction of the legally available working forest is not truly available because of either a lack of landowner interest in logging or a range of social, economic, and biophysical limitations, including steep slopes and distance from the nearest improved roads. This problem of effectively unavailable forestland is particularly acute in areas with high population densities and small parcel sizes. In effect, unabated forest growth on these unmanaged lands is masking the very heavy harvesting occurring on the truly available working forests.

There has also been a sea change in the ownership of working forestlands in the Northeast, particularly in the far north. Most dramatic has been the rise of timberland as an option for diversification of investment portfolios. Between 1980 and 2005 an acreage equal to over 50 percent of the forestland in the four northern forest states of New York, Vermont, New Hampshire, and Maine changed ownership, with much of it divested by the traditional vertically structured forest products companies and sold to investment firms. These were either timber investment management organizations or more broadly structured real estate investment trusts.[5] After being held by timber companies for much of the last century, these lands are typically now being bought, some fraction of the timber is logged, and then the property is sold to a new investment firm every ten to fifteen years. Needless to say, this has raised lots of eyebrows within the traditional forestry community, where sustainable management was previously thought of in terms of many decades to a century or more.

This change in the nature of ownership of large tracts of commercial timberland is playing out across the country. The majority of the forestland of the nine northeastern states, however, is still held in much smaller family forests. Indeed, the Northeast is distinctive in the low fraction of working forestland in public ownership:[6] only 4 percent of working forestland is owned by the federal government, and state and local governments control only an additional 13 percent. Of the remaining 83 percent of potential working forests, roughly 70 percent is in private, noncorporate holdings. Combine all of these numbers, and family forests represent more than half of the working forestland in the Northeast. And in the more fragmented forests of southern New England the proportion is much higher.

Foresters have traditionally focused most of their attention and research on developing methods to manage individual stands. This is usually done in the context of a well-defined set of silvicultural systems, of which clear-cutting, or even-aged management in foresters' parlance, is just one. But I've come to question the relevance of these by now largely academic designations for any given harvest. Clear-cutting is easy to define and has the added advantage that decades of research have gone into what are known as growth and yield studies that allow prediction of how soon and how much can be harvested in the next clear-cut. These sorts of calculations were at the center of planning by a timber or paper mill to ensure that their lands could maintain a steady and adequate supply of logs or fiber. The shift to partial harvesting presents a consulting forester with an enormous range of decisions about what fraction of the biomass of a stand to take in any given harvest, which individual trees to harvest and with what spacing, and when to plan the next harvest. And the divestment of commercial forestland means that harvest decisions are no longer dictated by mill owners taking a long-term perspective on their own timber supply.

Yet if individual harvests can be almost infinitely variable, their aggregate effects on the forest landscape can be assessed via the same approaches ecologists use to characterize and study natural disturbance regimes. And as the forest inventory data reveal, logging is far and away the most important disturbance in eastern forests. The first step in the description of any disturbance regime is a statistical analysis of the factors that determine the frequency and intensity of individual disturbances. For severe winds, the most common natural disturbance in northeastern forests, this is largely a function of climate and to a lesser extent the physical and ecological features that determine how susceptible a stand is to wind damage. But logging is fundamentally a result of human decisions. While the condition of the forest has a lot to do with decisions about whether and how much to log, social and economic factors are just as important.

The US Forest Service network of forest inventory plots has been invaluable in teasing apart the importance of these factors. For example, road building is a significant cost in any logging operation. So it's not a surprise that stands close to improved roads have a higher probability of being logged. There has been a lot of concern among foresters about the issue of parcelization, or the subdivision of forestland into smaller and smaller individual ownerships. The concern here is basically the problem of economy of scale. At some minimum size, the potential gross revenue from a harvest is simply too small to cover the fixed costs of the logging operation. There is indeed some evidence that small parcels are less frequently logged, but our analyses suggest that loggers have figured out a way to profitably operate in even small landholdings. Small parcels also tend to be located in areas with high population density, and there is evidence that as population density increases, the frequency of logging decreases. Such evidence may reflect differences in the expectations and interests of suburban versus rural forest owners, but I suspect it also reflects social pressure related to neighbors' concerns about the environmental and aesthetic impacts of logging. A recent study of forest harvests over a thirty-year period in Massachusetts found that increasing distance from Boston was one of the best predictors of the likelihood that a stand would be logged. Finally, one of the biggest factors determining the likelihood that a stand will be logged is simply the nature of the ownership. Privately owned forests in the Northeast are twice as likely to be logged as publicly owned forests, that is, approximately 3 percent of forest area harvested in any given year in the former and 1.5 percent in the latter. And among private forest owners, logging is 25 percent more likely in corporate-owned forests than on private woodlands (3.6%/yr versus 2.9%/yr).[7]

The net effects of all of these factors determine the relative proportion of forests in different successional stages (see fig. 15). Ecologists and foresters alike have traditionally thought of individual stands as having an age, one dating from the last catastrophic natural disturbance or the last clear-cut. But the harvest regimes recorded in the inventory data make it clear that stand age is not a meaningful concept for most northeastern forests since biomass is repeatedly set back by selective logging or natural disturbances like wind or ice storms that only affect a fraction of the canopy. It has been hard, however, to shake the desire to group forests by some measure of their stage in secondary succession. The most obvious alternative to age is simply total tree biomass. I have chosen arbitrary limits in figure 15 to define early-, mid-, and late-successional stands as well as old-growth forests. The effects of the intensive harvests in Maine are readily apparent. By my definition one-third of

Maine's forests are early successional, with tree biomass of less than fifty metric tons per hectare. The figure is only 10 percent for the rest of the Northeast. Mid- and late-successional stands dominate outside of Maine. For the nine northeastern states as a whole, including Maine, only 7 percent of forests meet my admittedly simple definition of old-growth (250 metric tons/ hectare), and in Maine only 1 percent of forests have reached that status.[8] While the regrowth of forest cover in the Northeast over the past century has been remarkable, it is still worth contrasting current conditions with what would have been present prior to European settlement. Given what we know about natural disturbances in the region, both the early- and mid-successional stages would have been exceedingly rare in a landscape where old-growth status would have been by far the most common condition.

My colleagues and I have used our models of northeastern forest dynamics to ask what the consequences of the current harvest regimes will be for the future abundance of the successional stages.[9] Those analyses tell us that if harvest regimes stay the same, it will take roughly one hundred years for the distribution of successional stages to stabilize. At that point average forest biomass will have increased by 45 percent from the current mean of 129 to over 166 metric tons per hectare (see fig. 15). Early-successional conditions will become less common, approximately 8 percent of the landscape, with most of those forests found in Maine. But given the frequent partial harvests found in all forest types, less than 20 percent of the landscape will reach the high biomass expected in old-growth conditions. Most of those forests will be found in New York on lands reserved from logging as part of the state's Forest Preserve. Overall, just over half of all northeastern forests will be in the combined late-successional/old-growth condition. This is much closer to the landscape that existed prior to European settlement but is still very different from it.

Our analyses are to a large degree an exercise in projecting the logical future consequences of the current logging regimes. Logging is not only the most frequent and intense disturbance in eastern forests, however, but also the most subject to change over time. There is reason to believe that wind disturbance regimes could intensify under climate change, and as I outlined in chapter 5 the natural fire regime has all but disappeared due to human diligence in fire suppression. But neither wind nor fire regimes are subject to the vagaries of economic and social forces that will shape the future of the logging regimes in northeastern forests. Something as simple as a change in consumer taste for the color of kitchen cabinets—what I think of as the Martha Stewart effect—can transform harvest practices. The current interest in light-colored cabinets has shifted harvest pressure from species like red oak and black cherry to sugar and red maple. Red maple (soft maple to a forester) has always brought lower prices than the harder wood of sugar maple and was often relegated to low-value uses like shipping pallets. But as the most common tree species in eastern North America, red maple is plentiful, and there is a lot of it to choose from. It can have the same kind of extravagant figure, both tiger and bird's-eye grain, found in its more pricey cousin. Even the distinctive discoloration, or spalting, that is common in red maple has become a virtue and is selected for by some furniture makers.

Other, more profound currents at work could alter the future of logging regimes in northeastern forests. It has been recognized for many years that carbon sequestered by forest regrowth in the eastern United States has been an important offset to greenhouse gas emissions. Some studies have suggested that the era of carbon sequestration in eastern forests is nearly at an end, as maturing forests become saturated. Our analyses and modeling of the forest inventory data indicate just the opposite. Outside of Maine under its current intensive harvests, the average biomass of the trees in northeastern forests and therefore total carbon sequestered will increase significantly before stabilizing in roughly one hundred years under current harvest regimes (see fig. 15).[10]

But two very different currents, both of which are driven by concern about climate change, could alter that course. On the one hand, forest-based biofuels could, at least in principle, become a sustainable, carbon-neutral alternative to fossil fuels.[11] Many states in the Northeast have set very aggressive goals for renewable energy, and most of those plans have at least implicitly assumed that logging will increase to provide the additional biomass needed so that forest biofuels will be a meaningful part of the mix. States and the federal government have created a variety of economic incentives to promote the development of forest biomass energy. It's fair to say that this move triggered a lot of alarm and opposition from environmental groups. It's also fair to say that the rise of cheap natural gas took the wind out of the sails for the construction of new large-scale forest biomass energy facilities in the Northeast. The story has been quite different in the southeastern US, where demand from Europe has produced an export-driven boom in forest harvest for production of wood pellets to co-fire with fossil fuel plants in Great Britain and Europe.

If the goal, however, is to offset fossil fuel emissions of carbon dioxide, then as long as forests still have the capacity to sequester more carbon there is little question that leaving the biomass in the forest is more effective than converting it to biomass energy. Wood has a very low energy density, and it's wet. The amount of fossil fuel emissions offset by combustion of a forest feedstock varies enormously depending on the technology used. I've done the calculation under a variety of scenarios, as have many other researchers. The bottom line always appears to be that more carbon is released per unit of useable energy from wood than from even inefficient fossil fuels like coal. So it takes more than one ton of forest carbon emitted from a biomass energy feedstock to offset a ton of carbon emitted from a fossil fuel. But allowing a forest to increase carbon storage by one ton is a direct 1:1 offset to a fossil fuel emission. So if the only policy goal is to offset fossil fuel emissions, then carbon sequestration wins out over forest biomass energy.[12]

For most of the past century forest owners have been providing the public benefit of sequestering carbon in their forests without financial compensation. The emergence in the past decade of a nascent market in domestic forest carbon offsets has the potential to thoroughly transform not just the economics of forest ownership but also the whole practice of silviculture in the Northeast. As much as half of the harvest in northern forests consists of low-grade wood destined for the shrinking number of paper mills in the region or is used as a feedstock for biomass energy as either firewood, by passing through a pellet mill, or being taken directly to one of the few large-scale wood-fired electricity generation stations in the region. Landowners typically receive no more than several dollars a ton for this material. That same amount of wood could bring the landowner two to as much as ten times as much money if left alive in the forest and marketed as a carbon offset.[13] The market for domestic forest carbon offsets is still in its infancy and typically imposes long-term compliance costs on the landowner to ensure that the carbon sequestration is effectively permanent. On the plus side this arrangement also means that carbon offset deals impose far stricter limitations than any of the existing forest certification programs to ensure that landowners maintain or increase the stocking in their forests. As in the case of the major forest certification programs, the paperwork and compliance requirements for forestry offset programs generally mean that currently only large landowners have access to this market.

If a tree wouldn't meet the standards for a high-quality sawlog and a landowner would receive much more money to leave it alive in the woods rather than cut it down, why would the landowner harvest the tree? The traditional answer from a consulting forester or an academic silviculturalist would be that by removing the low-grade tree you could release from competition any nearby potentially high-value trees, thereby increasing the rate of production of high-value sawlogs. There is certainly logic to this argument. I have spent years developing quantitative models to assess the strength of competition between neighboring trees, and there is no question that competition matters. But the strength of competition depends on the identity of the neighbor, how far away it is, and how big the neighbor is relative to the size of the tree you're trying to promote. The patterns are complex enough and the question new enough that I have not yet seen any analyses that can accurately weigh the economic pros and cons of removing versus leaving individual low-grade trees.

And while a tree may be considered low-grade as a timber resource loaded on a truck, that does not mean it has little ecological benefit or function when left in the woods, either alive or as a standing dead tree or downed deadwood. One argument for removing low-grade trees drives me to distraction. Removing high-grade trees and leaving just low-grade trees as seed trees, the argument goes, will result in a new generation of low-grade trees. The assumption, backed by neither logic nor data, is that there is a heritable genetic basis for low-grade timber quality. I suspect that this reasoning grew out of the opposite and more plausible argument that there might be a genetic component to really high-quality trees that could be passed on to the next generation. But low-grade in northeastern forests is a condition largely driven by damage and wounds received through the life of a tree. In many northern forests one of the most common causes of damage was from the scraping of bark near the base of the trees as skidders dragged logs out of the woods in harvests fifty years ago. It's hard to blame tree genetics for this fate.[14]

In one issue tree genetics and timber quality do clearly intersect. Beech bark disease is a complex consisting of a scale insect that bores tiny feeding tubes through the characteristically smooth beech bark, which then allows a fungal pathogen to invade the inner bark. A small fraction of beech trees are genetically resistant to the disease complex as a result of low contents in their bark of several amino acids the scale insect needs in order to thrive.[15] The disease has ravaged northeastern populations of the American beech for over a century. Damage from the complex builds up over time on a susceptible beech tree, and the cankers typically kill the tree before it can get to maturity and merchantable size. The North American species of beech, however, reproduces prolifically from root sprouts. To make matters worse, research has shown that wounding of beech roots, as routinely happens during a timber harvest, can stimulate even more sprouting. The net result of all this is what is technically known as beech hell: dense thickets of small beech that sprout after a harvest, most of which will start developing cankers before they reach merchantable size.

Foresters in the Northeast have known about beech bark disease for a hundred years. But beech has never been particularly valuable as a timber species, and I have long suspected that the early lack of concern about the disease reflected a view that beech was a low-value and therefore undesirable tree that was a strong competitor of more commercially important species. In the past thirty years, as the disease has spread west to Michigan and south to North Carolina, pathologists and entomologists have begun searching in earnest for means to control either the insects or the pathogens. The silvicultural responses to beech bark disease, however, have largely focused on trying to reduce the abundance of beech in forests where it has been dominant for thousands of years. Selective applications of herbicides to the stumps of cut beech trees have been largely abandoned due to costs. There has been a resurgence of interest, however, in the use of broad-spectrum herbicides to kill essentially all woody vegetation left after a harvest, in the hope of resetting the forest to a different mix of species with less beech. There also appears to be a belief that clear-cutting can at least reduce dominance by beech by maximizing the opportunities for less shade-tolerant species to get established. I have seen little evidence that either approach is effective, and both approaches represent very crude tools at best. I am glad to see that no one has seriously proposed trying to eliminate the more than 90 percent of beech trees and roots systems that are genetically susceptible to the disease complex in order to allow the population to rebuild from the small numbers of resistant individuals. Recovery of beech populations under that scenario would require millennia. If an effective biological control agent for either the scale insect or the fungal pathogen is found, on the other hand, the current generation of beech saplings and small trees that are too small to have developed cankers yet could grow to maturity disease-free within a century. Sadly, I'm not sure many foresters are all that excited by the possibility of the resurrection of this iconic northern tree.

All of these currents have convinced me that there is a desperate need for a new forestry in the Northeast. It will likely need to be very different in the northern hardwood- and conifer-dominated forests of the north than in the currently oak-dominated forests of southern portions of the region, if only because of the disparate patterns of landownership, parcel size, and human population density in the two regions. Carbon offset markets offer a clear incentive to explore whether light, selective logging can be refined into something traditional foresters no longer consider poor management that dooms a forest to lower and lower grade trees but instead promotes high-value trees while also providing the wide range of ecological and social benefits that mature forests provide. One of the greatest challenges will likely be in developing new markets for high-value timber, particularly markets that make use of the resource locally and thereby realize the obvious local economic benefits those types of new markets could bring. While the technology for timber harvesting has changed dramatically in the past several decades, with highly mechanized equipment now making it possible to selectively harvest a stand while causing little damage to the trees left behind for the next harvest, that technology requires enormous capital investment. As a result, it is rarely used in timber harvests in the small parcels that dominate the working forest landscape of southern New England. I'm beginning to wonder if the future of forestry in those small parcels lies in a return to the use of draft horses. And perhaps the biggest question facing forestry in the southern oak forests continues to be this one: will we be watching the slow but inexorable decline in the abundance of oaks or will that tide be reversed somehow?

8

Change Is in the Air

As I mentioned in the introduction, on December 7, 1986, the *New York Times* carried an article with the headline "Sugar Maple Faces Extinction Threat." According to forestry experts, the article stated, "the sugar maple tree is threatened with extinction in the Northeast unless drastic environmental protection measures are taken." It went on to assert that this state of affairs "follows a rapid decline in the tree population caused, according to environmental researchers, by acid rain and other pollution." Imagine my surprise. Two years earlier I had finished research for my doctoral degree comparing the ecology of sugar maple and beech, two of the most common trees in northern forests. While beech bark disease had been slowly working its way south from the Maritime Provinces of Canada for eighty years, the maples I studied seemed to be the picture of health.

The sensitivity of many tree species to acute air pollution was and is indisputable. One of my college roommates at Montana State University was from the town of Anaconda, the site of the smelter for the copper company of the same name. The mountain downwind of the smelter was denuded of trees. As early as the 1950s tree species known to be particularly sensitive to air pollution were being proposed for planting in cities to serve as sentinels of air quality. By the early 1980s chronic low levels of air pollution were suspected in a series of widespread diebacks of such species as red spruce at high elevations in the northeastern United States and other conifers in European forests.

The devastating effects of acid rain on aquatic ecosystems were equally indisputable.[1] Yet officials opposed to dealing with the issue were typically happy to fund new research, arguing that more study was needed before action could be taken. There was far less certainty that acid rain was a factor in symptoms observed in forests in the northeastern United States and western Europe. As part of the broader effort to assess the ecological effects of acid rain under the National Acid Precipitation Assessment Program, a Forest Response Program was initiated in 1985. Over the next five years it channeled large amounts of research funding to the question of the effects of acid rain on forest health. The program ended in controversy in 1990, and the *New York Times* ran an article titled "Acid Rain Report Unleashes a Torrent of Criticism."[2] Legislation to amend the Clean Air Act was being debated in Congress, and scientists worried that official summaries from the program were watered down by political considerations. But five years of intensive research uncovered only inconclusive evidence implicating acid rain in forest decline, and there was no scientific consensus over what caused the dieback and decline symptoms in either red spruce or sugar maple.

Outside the pressure cooker of big science, preoccupation about the long-term effects of acid rain on forests persisted, and scientists are getting closer to understanding just how those effects might play out. For example, survival of sugar maple seedlings is particularly sensitive to the supply of calcium in the soil, and there is evidence that chronic acid rain can deplete this critical soil nutrient. It was also thought that acid deposition was mobilizing aluminum in the soils of high-elevation forests and that this was interfering with calcium uptake by red spruce, making their needles more sensitive to injury in winter. Nonetheless, almost thirty years later sugar maple is still the second most abundant tree species in eastern forests, and although many red spruce trees did die during the 1980s, thickets of young spruce saplings are now common in northeastern forests. Whatever nexus of factors was responsible for the visible damage to red spruce trees at high elevations during the 1980s, a new study has reported "the surprising growth resurgence of red spruce in the Northern Forest" and attributes the recovery at least in part to a decline in acid rain.[3]

The Clean Air Act Amendments of 1990 were remarkably successful in reducing the emissions of sulfur dioxide that became sulfuric acid in the atmosphere. But that legislation did less to curb the emissions of nitrogen oxides that react to become nitric acid in rainfall. While deposition of nitric acid has been slowly declining in much of the northeastern United States, the inputs remain a significant concern. At first blush the input of nitrogen might be seen as a net positive, since it is widely assumed to be the most common limiting nutrient in northeastern forests. And in fact a number of studies have concluded that forest productivity has been enhanced by this fertilization. But as is true of almost all changes in the environment, there are winners and losers. The roots of tree species form symbioses with different types of soil fungi. Many of the tree species with the form known as ectomycorrhizae have higher mortality rates in areas with high nitrogen deposition. The oaks are prominent in this group. Conversely, species like the maples with the alternative form in their roots (endomycorrhizal fungi) often show higher growth and survival as a result of modest levels of nitrogen deposition.[4]

The nitrogen oxides that are a part of acid rain are also a link in the production of ground-level ozone, a powerful oxidant with effects on both plants and animals. Tree species like black cherry and yellow birch that are highly sensitive to ground-level ozone can show acute symptoms, such as lesions on leaves and more chronic reductions in growth. Paradoxically, although automobile emissions in cities are a major source of nitrogen oxides, the resulting production of ozone takes time—specifically, sunlight and heat—and areas downwind of major cities often have higher ozone levels than the cities. On the other hand, many tree species, notably oaks in eastern forests, can release large quantities of isoprenes—volatile organic compounds—on hot summer days. The combination of isoprenes and nitrogen oxides is a potent recipe for ground-level ozone and smog. This chemistry is at the root of Ronald Reagan's widely reported and ridiculed assertion in 1981 that "trees cause more pollution than automobiles do." As many commentators noted, the isoprenes alone don't result in ozone, so the statement ignores the crucial role of human emissions of nitrogen oxides. But there is ample evidence that ground-level ozone can be particularly acute downwind of the large areas of oak forests in the southern Appalachians. In one of the more perverse results, the tree species that release large quantities of isoprenes also tend to be less sensitive to ozone damage. A computer simulation study suggests that long-term ozone exposure could promote these isoprene-emitting but ozone-insensitive tree species, making the problem even worse over time.[5] Nonetheless, direct evidence of pervasive effects of ozone exposure on either forest composition or productivity remains elusive. There is some tantalizing evidence that genetic variation in ozone tolerance of individuals within some tree species is reduced in areas with polluted air. Over time, only pollution-tolerant genotypes persist. We don't know what other traits might have been lost with the disappearance of pollution-sensitive genotypes.

While acid rain and ozone are what first come to mind when we think about air pollution in eastern forests, the most pervasive and so far intractable change in the chemistry of the atmosphere has been the increase in the concentration of carbon dioxide. The overriding concern has been with impacts of rising carbon dioxide on our climate. But carbon dioxide is also a plant nutrient, and changes in carbon dioxide concentrations could, at least in principle, have wide-ranging effects on tree physiology independent of the effects of changes in climate. Plants face an unavoidable trade-off between taking up the carbon dioxide needed for photosynthesis and losing water vapor at the same time. Carbon dioxide is taken up and water vapor simultaneously lost through stomates, small pores on the surfaces of leaves. Closing these pores minimizes water loss but at the same time impedes taking up carbon dioxide. If the concentration of carbon dioxide in the atmosphere increases, then more of it can be taken up per unit of water vapor loss. Species from arid environments have an impressive array of adaptations to minimize water loss and maximize the amount of photosynthesis per unit of water lost. Eastern forests are not typically thought of as arid environments, but there is good evidence that water loss is an important stress on eastern trees during periodic summer droughts or on thin soils with little capacity for storing water. So at least in principle rising atmospheric carbon dioxide concentrations could increase water-use efficiency and rates of photosynthesis in eastern trees.

Tests of those hypotheses have consumed millions of dollars and entire research careers over the past thirty years. Early studies used either growth chambers in laboratories or small open-top chambers in nature where carbon dioxide concentrations could be experimentally manipulated while minimizing changes in climate or other factors. Results were mixed. Among northeastern tree species the growth of seedlings of only a few species, notably red oak and sugar maple, was enhanced under highly elevated carbon dioxide levels. By the mid-1990s there were mounting concerns about whether these small chambers could accurately reflect what would happen in the real world, and small chambers can't test effects on large trees. An elegant but expensive solution was the development of "free air carbon dioxide enrichment" facilities (fig. 17). These consisted of rings of nozzles placed around groups of trees within a forest. Computers responding to wind direction and speed would then control the release of carbon dioxide at the right locations and rates to maintain a desired concentration of carbon dioxide around the trees. One of the earliest facilities was established by Duke University in 1994 to study responses of loblolly pines (*Pinus taeda*). A facility in Tennessee has measured responses in sweetgum (*Liquidambar styraciflua)* trees, and a facility in Wisconsin has measured responses in a more diverse set of northern hardwood species. The Wisconsin site included the ability to simultaneously manipulate both carbon dioxide and ozone.

It is not a coincidence that this research was funded by the US Department of Energy, with at least the tacit support of the energy industry. There was hope that rising carbon dioxide would stimulate higher rates of productivity and carbon sequestration in forests, providing at least some offset for greenhouse gas emissions. It is fair to say that after twenty-five years of intensive study there is little support for that idea. Tree growth rates in some of the sites initially increased but subsequently declined as part of complex feedbacks operating on a wide range of ecological processes. To be fair, I would add that an enormous

Figure 17. The free air carbon dioxide enrichment (FACE) facility at the Duke Forest in North Carolina. The towers release carefully controlled amounts of carbon dioxide into the atmosphere around the loblolly pine trees for study of the effects of elevated carbon dioxide levels on a wide range of ecosystem processes. Photo credit: Adrien Finzi.

amount has been learned about both tree physiology and forest ecosystem processes along the way. Effort seems to be moving away from massive investment in these field studies toward attempts to use detailed results from the experiments in computer simulation models. A fundamental challenge remains, however: we have data for only a few tree species under a limited range of environmental conditions.

My best guess is that there may indeed be some potential for rising carbon dioxide to increase overall forest productivity and carbon sequestration, but not by very much and not in the way most researchers expected. One of the primary criticisms of early, small, open-topped chamber studies was that they were limited to measurements on tree seedlings rather than on adult trees. But forest productivity turns out to be unexpectedly sensitive to seedling growth and survival. And some of the compensatory processes that limited growth responses of mature trees in the larger experiments may not apply to seedlings. A more prolific understory in the forest is faster to replace a canopy tree that dies, the net result being a slightly more productive forest overall. I have to confess that I have little confidence in anyone's ability to rigorously test this hypothesis. Colleagues and I advanced this idea based on computer simulations over twenty years ago but have never had the data needed to validate those model predictions.[6]

There are important lessons in all of this research for thinking about how tree species and forests respond to novel stresses and changes in the environment. The first is a resounding demonstration that consequences at the level of leaves or even whole plant physiology don't simply scale up to predict changes in tree populations or forest ecosystem properties. The study of effects of rising carbon dioxide levels, in particular, has revealed a complex web of compensatory mechanisms that dampen or even reverse any direct, immediate benefits for leaf water use and photosynthesis. And syntheses of the results from the experiments that have manipulated carbon dioxide concentrations readily admit that there is enough variation in responses both within and among species that positive and negative effects on different individual trees and species could cancel each other out. More generally, almost all of this research has been done by either plant physiologists or ecosystem scientists. But changes in forest structure and function are fundamentally a result of demography, that is, changes in birth, growth, and death among all of the component species. And with few exceptions the research on effects of air pollution has focused only on the growth of individuals and usually only on a limited range of sizes, ignoring the more critical life history processes of birth and death; what's more, it has been conducted in the absence of interactions with many other species.

A second lesson, one of the silver linings in this chemical cloud, was that we needed much better long-term monitoring of forest health so that we could detect meaningful trends in the status of our tree species. Just as important, the tracking needed to be able to keep us from swinging at pitches in the dirt, particularly anecdotal reports of visible symptoms of injury to tree leaves that didn't translate into meaningful changes in the demography of tree species. Fortunately, the foundation for such a program was in place long before concerns about air pollution. Since the 1930s the US Forest Service has been recording forest conditions across the United States in its Forest Inventory and Analysis network. The motivation for the network came from concerns about the sustainability of the nation's timber supply. That concern remains, but by 1988 legislation formally expanded the focus of the inventory "[to address] matters that relate to atmospheric pollution" and "to monitor long-term trends in the health and productivity of domestic forest ecosystems." Over the past twenty years the forest inventory network and the associated Forest Health Monitoring network have become valuable resources for scientists. And while it is critical to track the responses of forests, it is also vital to have good long-term data on the chemistry of the atmosphere. Air quality monitoring tends to be concentrated in urban areas, for reasons having to do with human health. But since 1978 a nationwide network of sites has been measuring the chemistry of the atmosphere. Originally it focused on the acidity of rainfall but eventually also incorporated measures of dry deposition of aerosol particles. The network is extensive enough to provide reasonable estimates of both acid deposition and total nitrogen deposition, even in remote forested areas.[7] The atmosphere is a complex mélange, with a chemistry that varies dramatically in space and time as a result of natural processes and the many diverse activities of humans. The silos of research on different pollutants have traditionally viewed them as stresses, a perspective that obscures the fact that atmospheric chemistry is a fundamental feature of the forest environment, one of the most dynamic at that. Translating from either visible or biochemical markers of stress at the leaf or even whole plant level to changes in the demography of tree species remains a major challenge. This is especially true when the stresses of air pollution are combined with effects of other agents like insect defoliation and drought. The most unambiguous effects of air pollution on eastern forests can be traced to current levels of nitrogen deposition. That research shows clear winners and losers among the regions' tree species, with effects on both growth and survival that are large enough to translate into immediate impacts on forest productivity and potentially significant long-term changes in species composition. But how this all will play out has as much to do with politics, legislation, and environmental regulation as with science. Regulations aimed at reducing nitrogen pollution, with their obvious benefits to both human health and the environment, have been tied up by legal challenges and administrative roadblocks for years. There is some reason to hope for meaningful reductions over the next decade or two, but, like so many of the environmental changes that humans have wrought, the long-term legacies of one hundred years of air pollution are still clouded and uncertain.

9
New and Unwelcome Passengers

odern genetic methods are revolutionizing our understanding of evolution, but something as simple as geographic isolation remains one of the most powerful causes of speciation and the remarkable diversity of organisms that can be found around the globe. Humans have been ever more frenetically erasing that isolation, both deliberately and inadvertently. The temperate forests of eastern North America are assumed to be the descendants, along with closely related forests in Europe and temperate regions of Asia, of an ancient flora that was continuous across far northern latitudes during the much warmer late Cretaceous period more than sixty-six million years ago. As the climate cooled and the northern continents separated and drifted southward, their plants and animals were isolated from each other and evolved and diverged into distinctly different species. Today, if you walk through a forest in the northern Japanese island of Hokkaido you will find members of most of the common genera of trees found in the northeastern United States. But instead of our six species of maples (in the genus *Acer*) there are nine species in Hokkaido, even more to the south on the main island of Honshu, and over ninety species on the mainland in China.[1] The striking differences in the diversity of modern-day tree species in the temperate forests of Asia, North America, and Europe have been studied for over a century. Europe comes in last, with extinction due to lack of refugia from Pleistocene glaciations often taking the blame—the Mediterranean Sea sits in the way of southern migration during the ice ages. China wins by a landslide, in part because of ample avenues for southward migration during the Pleistocene, but even more so because of a strong terrestrial connection to moist tropical and subtropical forests and the greater diversity of tropical lineages that have found their way northward into its temperate forests. Eastern North America comes in a distant second. Ample refugia existed south of the glacial maximum during the Pleistocene, but we lack the strong land connection to moist subtropical and tropical forests due to the presence of the Caribbean Sea.

These differences are fascinating to me and mean that I feel right at home walking in the woods in Europe or temperate Asia. But they have much more profound importance in understanding the flood of nonnative plants currently found in our forests, fields, and wetlands. There are between three and four thousand species of vascular plants in the state of New York, depending on who's counting, and roughly 35 percent of them are nonnatives. Studies in other northeastern states give similar estimates of both the total number of species and the fraction that are nonnative. The vast majority of the introduced plant species are naturalized, that is, well established but not spreading rapidly. A smaller but still significant number of those are invasive and spreading rapidly. This problem is not unique to North America. The British Isles have fewer than three thousand vascular plant species, and 43 percent of them are nonnative.

Virtually all of these introductions come from the movement of plants across the mid-latitude regions of the northern hemisphere, for the perhaps obvious reason that their climates and ecosystems are so similar.[2]

We often complain about being swamped by European weeds, and there is in fact some asymmetry in the numbers of herbaceous species that have become invasive or simply naturalized when transferred across the Atlantic. European settlers brought agricultural weeds with them, presumably in hay carried to feed livestock en route. The early botanists were also busily sending seeds of North American species back to Europe, both for ornamental gardens and as new food crops. But while active and abandoned agricultural fields were rare in the Northeast before European settlement, there had been millennia for species to adapt to active agriculture in the same climate in Europe. So it's little surprise that there were more species suitable for transport from Europe to the new agricultural landscape of America than vice versa.

We aren't anywhere close to blameless, however, in the global plague of invasive species. Black locust is a tree native to the Ohio Valley. It was highly valued by early American farmers and was actively dispersed outside of its original range in the United States, in part because of the decay resistance of fence posts made from its numerous root sprouts. It is believed to be the first North American tree species introduced to Europe. In addition to its durable wood, its flowers were a source of prized honey. It's also a legume and fixes nitrogen in its roots, making it well adapted to colonizing highly degraded soils in postindustrial sites. Today, it is one of the most common trees in central Europe and dominates almost a quarter of forests in Hungary.[3] Our native black cherry is highly invasive in the Low Countries of western Europe. Foresters here would probably be delighted if it was more common, given its high value as a timber species. Unfortunately, in Europe it rarely has the nice straight form it shows in its native habitat. Our northeastern goldenrods are members of a large genus (*Solidago*) of herbaceous species, most of which are native to North America. One of our most common goldenrods, *Solidago canadensis*, is reported to have been introduced to Shanghai in 1935 and is by now a rapidly spreading, serious invader across eastern China. I have seen dense fields of it in fallow rice paddies outside Tokyo, growing to almost twice the height I've ever seen it in the United States.

In the spirit of never letting a crisis go to waste, there has been an enormous body of often elegant ecological research on what determines the invasiveness of a species in a new setting and the factors that determine how susceptible a native ecosystem is to invasion. Many factors are at work, but an important attribute of many successful invaders is the absence of their natural enemies, particularly pathogens and insects, in the new habitat. Native soil pathogens appear to play an important role in limiting the abundance of black cherry in northeastern forests. One of the reasons the species is so successful at invading forests in Europe is that aggressive forms of the pathogen, a damping off disease that can kill seedlings, do not appear to be present in European soils.[4]

Much of the research on introduced plants has focused on species of open and early successional habitats and species adapted to colonize following disturbance. This makes sense given that most of the nonnative plants of the Northeast are species of open habitats and are presumably shade intolerant. The traits that make a species capable of aggressively spreading in those habitats—producing large numbers of seeds with long-distance dispersal and rapid growth in high light—are almost by definition the traits that are normally associated with early successional and weedy life histories. The focus on invaders as early successional species can be traced to the nature of most introductions. Almost three-quarters of the nonnative species established in the Finger Lakes Region of New York over the past seventy-five years escaped from cultivation, and most were deliberately introduced for their performance in open or high light environments. For woody plants the number is even higher: in North America 99 percent of all naturalized nonnative woody plants were deliberately introduced, either for landscaping or commercial forestry. Relatively few of those species were chosen because of their shade tolerance.[5]

This has led to the erroneous perception that closed forests are relatively immune to invasive species. It can't be a surprise that species introduced because they do well in open environments aren't particularly successful at invading a shaded forest understory. And while the list of introduced species in the Northeast that are shade tolerant is small (but growing), an alarmingly high percentage of them have become invasive in our forests.[6] All of this is by way of saying that introduced plant species are indeed a threat to the future of northeastern forests, but it is worth stepping back and assessing the actual ecological consequences of the spread of these nonnative plant species.

I noted in chapter 4 that forests that have reestablished on abandoned agricultural land are only slowly regaining their native understory species. Some of the more shade-tolerant nonnative shrubs, including Japanese barberry (*Berberis thunbergii*), burning bush (*Euonymous alatus*), and species of honeysuckles (in the genus *Lonicera*), are common in these forests. All of these species are readily dispersed by birds, but this fact also points to their habitat value for both birds and small mammals, particularly in stands where native shrubs have more slowly reestablished. It is probably heresy to say so, but in most cases I consider the addition of these nonnative species to be a net ecological benefit since without them there would be little in the shrub layer at all. That way of thinking, however, didn't stop me from pulling up the honeysuckles in the bit of woods on my property years ago. Looking back, I'm not sure why I bothered.

A pair of invasive, shade-tolerant herbaceous species, garlic mustard (*Alliaria petiolata*) and Japanese stiltgrass (*Microstegium vimineum*), are spreading rapidly into forest understories in the Northeast. I may be much more justified in my efforts to weed out the garlic mustard from my woods than the honeysuckles. Kristina Stinson and colleagues have discovered a toxic effect of compounds released from roots or decaying leaves of garlic mustard.[7] The compounds disrupt the critical mutualisms between native trees and one of the two main groups of fungi (arbuscular mycorrhizae) that colonize tree roots and aid in the uptake of nutrients. Our native trees that depend on a mutualism with that type of fungi include the maples, ashes, and black cherries. Experiments show that seedlings of these tree species are smaller and less numerous when grown in soil from stands that have been invaded by garlic mustard.

As scary as this sounds, it's not a foregone conclusion that garlic mustard foretells a grim fate for trees that rely on arbuscular mycorrhizae. We need to know much more about the extent and persistence of the effects on the fungi and tree seedlings as well as on adult trees under a much broader range of field conditions. In its native environment in Europe garlic mustard does not appear to suppress the mutualism, suggesting that the European fungi have evolved tolerance. Whether the North American fungi can rapidly do the same is unknown. So

I find it hard to generalize from these initial and quite limited experiments. But given all of the other factors that can lead to lack of tree regeneration in our forests, garlic mustard can't be helping.

Japanese stiltgrass is a more recent arrival in the Hudson River Valley where I live and is just starting to spread into the woods near me. The evidence for negative effects of stiltgrass on native species is less striking than that for garlic mustard but includes some of the same genre of chemically mediated (allelochemical) interactions. Stiltgrass can form dense patches in the understory. I suspect that this leads to an expectation that in addition to any allelochemical inhibition of native species, stiltgrass might simply crowd out existing native species or prevent the establishment of new tree seedlings or populations of native understory species. As in the case of garlic mustard, there is a growing body of controlled field experiments that show the potential of stiltgrass to indeed outcompete some native species.

I am skeptical, however, that stiltgrass is a major threat to the diversity or abundance of native herbs, shrubs, or trees. You can find dramatic photos on the internet of forests with an almost uniform understory of stiltgrass, but I suspect there was little if any native understory in those stands before its arrival. And it is far more commonly present in small but dense patches. Whether those patches will thin over time is unknown, as is whether native species, particularly shrubs, could colonize and overtop the stiltgrass. The bottom line for me is that the diversity and abundance of species in the understories of northeastern forests, even in the forests that did not suffer the bottleneck of an agricultural history, are not zero-sum games. The addition of a nonnative species, even one that is aggressively invading, does not inevitably imply a meaningful reduction in the diversity and abundance of native understory species.

The same is clearly not true of invasive nonnative tree species. You can only pack so many adult trees into a forest canopy. Establishment of nonnative trees in the canopy will necessarily come at the expense of the abundance of native tree species. Colleagues and I have looked in detail at the ecology of the two most common invasive tree species in forests of southern New England, Norway maple and tree of heaven.[8] The results of what I consider to be a fairly exhaustive set of field studies to incorporate the two species in our model of forest dynamics produced somewhat reassuring results. Both species, through very different life history strategies, are fully capable of invading forests on a broad range of soils. Tree of heaven is not shade tolerant but puts on more height growth in even fairly small canopy openings than any native tree species. It also releases an allelochemical compound from its roots that can reduce the growth of seedlings of some of the native tree species, at least when they try to grow within a meter or two of the stem of a tree of heaven. Norway maple, in contrast, would rate as one of the most shade-tolerant species in northeastern forests. It casts deeper shade than any other species at our study sites.

But neither species blankets a forest with seeds, and they are currently most often found spreading into forest stands from trees along roads—trees that likely established from seeds dispersed by automobiles. And, like the native species, they have to wait for some form of opening in the forest canopy before they can reach adult size and spread farther into woods. Under modest levels of natural disturbance or logging, our analyses suggest that both species will slowly but inexorably increase in abundance at the expense of native species but on timescales of a century or more rather than decades. And if I've learned anything it's that many factors could intervene in that time frame. A native fungus has been attacking tree of heaven in Pennsylvania, and early tests suggest it could be deployed as a biological control. Norway maple relies on arbuscular mycorrhizae, like its North American relatives. I know of no research, however, on how invasion by garlic mustard might alter the success of invasion by Norway maple.

I've focused on nonnative plants in northeastern forests largely because there are so many of them. But there is at least one group of invasive nonnative animals in northeastern forests worth considering: the lowly earthworms.[9] Forests north of the southern boundary of Pleistocene glaciers typically lacked native earthworms prior to European settlement, presumably because of slow northward migration of native North American species. A large number of earthworm species have been introduced subsequently from Europe and Asia, including the common nightcrawler (*Lumbricus terrestris*). Gardeners typically view them as beneficial because of their ability to mix and aerate the soil. Ecologists view them more generally as highly effective ecosystem engineers. Their most visually dramatic impact is the ability to eliminate the layer of leaf litter on the forest floor, leaving a surface of bare mineral soil.

I've talked elsewhere about the dichotomy between tree species such as maples and ashes, which shed nutrient-rich, rapidly decomposing leaf litter, and species such as the oaks and beech, which shed much more slowly decomposing leaf litter. The forest floor in a neighborhood dominated by maples and ashes typically has very thin, patchy leaf litter remaining by midsummer and little if any distinct surface layer of soil organic matter. Neighborhoods dominated by oaks and beeches, on the other hand, will have a thick layer of leaf litter over a distinct layer of slowly decomposing organic matter. These are fundamentally different ecosystems in a number of ways: in patterns of nutrient cycling, in soil microbial communities, and food webs of invertebrates and vertebrates like salamanders. The impacts of introduction of earthworms are most dramatic in the sites with an existing deep litter layer. But in both types of neighborhoods the forest floor can be transformed into a uniformly bare layer of mineral soil. Photos from forests in the upper Midwest of advancing wave fronts of earthworm invasion are positively creepy. As is true of any change in the environment, there are winners (few) and losers (many) in the aftermath.

Conservation departments in northern states have established education programs to encourage fishermen to not dump their bucket of nightcrawlers in the woods at the end of a day on the water. This will help slow the spread, but it's unlikely to stop it. And while there are lots of field studies documenting changes in the abundance of herbaceous species and tree seedlings due to the first invasion of earthworms, there is much less certainty about longer-term impacts. Seedlings of small-seeded species like hemlock and yellow birch are most often found established on a raised surface like a well-rotted log or the bare mineral soil of a tip-up mound, simply because they grow so little in their first year or two that they would be smothered by the slowly decomposing oak or beech leaves that accumulate in depressions. It's possible that those seedlings might become more abundant following establishment of earthworms. But the faster nutrient cycling in the wake of the earthworms could also benefit competitors like the maples. And in many of these invasions the dramatic changes wrought by the first wave of a new species can fade in their wake.

There is little question that invasive species are a constantly growing threat to ecosystems worldwide, and the threat appears to be widely recognized by the public. I see little hope of eliminating the threat but am heartened by the breadth of the commitment to dealing with it at so many levels, from volunteers in local nature preserves to federal agencies and global conservation groups.[10] And while it is clear that forests are not necessarily more resistant to invasion than other eco-systems, it seems clear to me that the immediacy of the threats in northeastern forests pales in comparison to the impacts of invasive species on our wetlands, rivers, and lakes.

The resources needed to fight this battle are not unlim-ited, and organizations have put a lot of thought into where and how to focus their efforts.[11] My sense is that the fight is concen-trated on three fronts. The first is clearly the early detection and, if possible, eradication when a known invasive reaches a new site. The second is on the almost perpetual need to control invasives on specific preserves, even when the preserve is as large as the six-million-acre Adirondack Park. The third, more personal, is the willingness of private landowners to take on the stewardship of their lands. I find that plucking out the second-year stems of garlic mustard in my woods before they can set seed is remarkably satisfying and actually quite effective. These efforts are not nearly as quixotic as they may sound. Much of the unique plant diversity in the northern forest landscape is concentrated in often tiny and unique geologic settings: the gems embedded in the firmament. In contrast, you can walk for weeks through northern forests and in the first thirty min-utes of the first day you will see the vast majority of the vascu-lar plant species you will encounter in the entire trek.[12] The gems are important enough that we can and should focus our efforts on protecting them.

10

A Far More Threatening Invasion

I t is a sad fact that the millions of years of geographic isolation that played such a central role in the evolution of species diversity in temperate forests have also made those species defenseless in the face of so many newly introduced insects and diseases. The global trade that over the past century has brought a constant stream of introduced plants has also been the source of the inadvertent but far more damaging introduction of a host of new forest pests and pathogens. The northeastern United States has the greatest number of destructive forest pests in the country.[1] The explanation is quite simple: insects and diseases that hitch a ride to a northeastern port on solid wood packing material or live plants from either Europe or temperate regions in Asia find new host trees species that are closely related to their hosts back home. The same insects and diseases arriving in the port of Los Angeles find fewer suitable hosts in southern California. The litany is truly depressing. I won't try to catalogue it here, but table 1 has a rogue's gallery of some of the most destructive introductions dating back over a century. The list of recently discovered pests and pathogens with potentially devastating impacts is far longer, and the pace of introductions, particularly for wood-boring insects, is accelerating. I think most forest ecologists would agree with me that these pests and pathogens represent the greatest current threat to northeastern forests.

The routes for these invasions are well known. A recent study estimated that close to 70 percent of the most damaging nonnative insects and diseases established in the United States over the past 150 years entered on imported live plants.[2] Other studies come to the same conclusion about the sources of the majority of forest pest and pathogen introductions in Europe. White pine blister rust is believed to have been introduced over 100 years ago on pine seedlings imported from Europe. The threat to the economic value of both eastern and western species of white pines was severe enough that it contributed to the passage of the Plant Quarantine Act of 1912 and also provided the motivation for decades of government efforts to eradicate native species of gooseberries and currants (in the genus *Ribes*), since those shrubs provided an alternate host for the fungus. While the threat to eastern white pine has abated over the past century, blister rust has emerged as a new threat to the iconic whitebark pine (*Pinus albicaulis*) of treeline in the Rocky Mountains, a species already reeling from the impacts of mountain pine beetles.

All imported plants are required to pass through inspection stations located at US ports of entry. There they are inspected by staff from the US Department of Agriculture's Animal and Plant Health Inspection Service (APHIS). I have enormous respect for the work they do, but they face an enormous and ever growing workload with what seems a minuscule workforce. A study has estimated that each of the approximately sixty-five full-time inspectors nationwide in 2010 was responsible for inspecting forty-three million plants per year.[3] Obviously they can examine only a fraction of the plants since there are thirty-

Table 1. A rogue's gallery of the most destructive introduced forest pests and pathogens in the northeastern United States. The US Department of Agriculture maintains websites that provide maps and descriptions of more than a hundred forest pests and pathogens nationwide. The list grows every year. In the Northeast a more complete table would include the sirex wood wasp, the southern pine beetle, oak wilt, thousand canker disease, balsam wooly adelgid, red pine scale, and the winter moth.

Pest or pathogen	Host tree species[a]	Mode of action	Date detected[b]	Impact[c]
Beech bark disease (scale insect plus fungal pathogen)	American beech	Cankers girdle the tree[d]	Late 1800s on live trees from Europe	A small fraction of trees are genetically resistant; otherwise, adult stems die back but can resprout from roots
Chestnut blight (fungal pathogen)	American chestnut	Cankers girdle the tree	Late 1800s on live trees from Asia	Few individuals survive to adulthood, stems die back, and often resprout
Dutch elm disease (fungal pathogen spread by bark beetles)	Both of our local species of elms (American and slippery elm)	Vascular wilt that plugs xylem (water-conducting tissues)	~1930 in Ohio[e] but first identified in the 1920s in the Netherlands	Has largely eliminated elms from dense populations in swamp forests, scattered individuals survive in uplands

(continued)

Table 1. (continued)

Pest or pathogen	Host tree species[a]	Mode of action	Date detected[b]	Impact[c]
Gypsy moth (a defoliating moth)	Very broad list of hosts[f]	Defoliation leads to reduction in growth, and mortality in stressed individuals	1869 as a potential alternative to silkworm moths	Is highly dependent on severity of other stresses on trees during defoliation events
Asian longhorned beetle	Maples, birches, poplars, and many others[g]	Larvae consume large quantities of wood while boring through branches and the trunk	1996 in Brooklyn, subsequent discovery in other locations in North America	Aggressive eradication programs have successfully limited the extent of known outbreaks
Hemlock woolly adelgid	Eastern and Carolina hemlocks	Sucking insect depletes a tree's reserves, leading to death	Found on museum collections from the 1950s in Virginia	Northern range limited by cold winter temperatures, widespread mortality south of that
Dogwood anthracnose (fungal pathogen)	Flowering dogwood	Branch dieback leading to death	1970s in the Northeast, presumably from Asia	All sizes, particularly in shaded environments

Emerald ash borer (wood boring beetle)	Most, if not all, species of ash[h]	Larvae bore beneath the bark, consuming cambium, phloem, and xylem	2002 in Michigan	Kills both saplings and adult trees by effectively girdling the tree; insects disperse very effectively
Butternut canker (fungal pathogen)	Butternut	Cankers girdle the tree	1967 in Wisconsin	Kills both saplings and adult trees

[a] Only the host tree species in the eastern United States are listed. Many of these pests and pathogens have a much broader range of host trees outside the eastern United States.

[b] New pests and pathogens are typically detected some years after they were first introduced. Researchers typically work backward once they are detected to determine when and where the original introduction happened.

[c] Whether or not the pest or pathogen kills all sizes or just some life history stages is a critical factor in its impact on population dynamics.

[d] Feeding holes created by the scale insect allow introduction of the fungus beneath the bark.

[e] Believed to have been introduced on logs imported to the United States from Europe.

[f] Will feed on almost all species of woody plants during severe outbreaks.

[g] The list is being refined as more outbreaks are studied.

[h] There is evidence that at least blue ash is somewhat resistant.

Sources: Web resources include the USDA Alien Forest Pest Explorer and the Forest Health Pest Portal. https://foresthealth.fs.usda.gov/portal; https://www.nrs.fs.fed.us/tools/afpe/maps/.

one million seconds in a year. It seems inevitable, at least in the absence of much greater funding, that inspections are at best a first line of defense. Indeed, that study estimated that over 70 percent of infestations would not be detected by standard inspections. The work of inspectors in the United States is supplemented by APHIS staff based overseas, and APHIS has instituted a number of new approaches to reducing the threat, including by creating a list of species of plants for which risk assessments of their potential to harbor new pests must be done before that plant species can be imported. As you might expect, there are economic forces that oppose any restrictions on this trade as well as real limitations in the ability of the scientific community to anticipate and quantify all of the potential risks.

The other major pathway for invasion has been from insects burrowed inside solid wood packaging. This has been the most likely route for wood-boring insects like the Asian longhorned beetle and the emerald ash borer, currently the two most economically devastating insect pests in northeastern forests. International standards are supposed to require either heat treatment or fumigation of solid wood used in pallets and packaging. But the treatments are clearly not fully effective, and it is widely assumed that some packaging is fraudulently stamped without ever having been treated. There are many alternatives to solid wood packaging that eliminate the risk of harboring forest pests, including plywood, oriented strand board, metal, and even recycled plastics. Analyses show clear and substantial net economic benefits from the current, if not completely effective, treatment standards and even greater economic benefits from switching to alternative materials.[4] But again, there are powerful economic interests behind the current use of solid wood packaging in international trade. Who knew that the National Wooden Pallet and Container Association had so many members and was such an effective lobby? This is another in the long list of cases in which an industry doesn't directly bear the true cost of their business.

It is cold comfort that we have not yet witnessed the outright extinction of any of our native tree species due to these introduced insects and diseases. While that is not out of the question, the most common fate is decimation of the populations of adult trees (see table 1). Scattered trees persist for a number of reasons: they become so rare that the insect or disease can't find them all; some life history stages, usually seedlings or saplings, are not as vigorously attacked; or some typically very small fraction of individuals are truly resistant. While best known as a beloved street tree, American elms were most abundant in floodplain forests across the eastern and midwestern United States and northward into the central Canadian provinces. But they and their relative the slippery elm also occur scattered throughout upland forests, particularly on soils with a moderately high pH. Dutch elm disease, a fungal vascular wilt disease, was first detected around 1927. It is believed to have been introduced on logs imported from Europe, where the disease had previously been described as attacking elms in the Netherlands (see table 1). It is spread by both native and introduced bark beetles. Once the beetles discover a swamp forest dominated by elms, the disease spreads rapidly throughout the stand. The beetles generally ignore seedlings and small elms, and even small elms can produce new seeds, so there are still often lots of elm seedlings and saplings in those floodplains. But mature trees are now largely a distant memory in those forests. The beetles are imperfect vectors for the disease, however, and scattered trees in the uplands are more likely to escape detection. Today, if you spend enough time walking in the uplands you can still come across rare but majestic mature elms.[5]

It is almost axiomatic in ecology that each species is a node in a complex web of interactions with other species and that decimation of even one node can ramify throughout the web. This is particularly true of tree species since, as I have argued earlier in this book, trees form the fabric of the ecological patchwork that is a forest. Animal ecologists who study the loss of top predators from a food web have coined the term "keystone species" to describe those whose loss cascades through the rest of the food web, changing the abundance of many other species. Plant ecologists who have studied the loss of tree species to pests and pathogens have coined the term "foundational species" to identify trees whose disappearance profoundly alters the environment in ways that transform ecosystem functions and propagate up through the ecological web of species in a forest.

The concept of a foundational tree species was first invoked to describe the ecological consequences of loss of eastern hemlock as a result of the combined impact of the hemlock woolly adelgid and the elongate hemlock scale.[6] It's not hard to see why. A hemlock grove has a distinctively shady understory year-round. The forest floor typically has a thick organic horizon of slowly decomposing hemlock needles, with an often sparse layer of herbaceous species and shrubs. Soils are typically acidic, with low rates of nitrogen cycling and correspondingly low rates of leakage of nitrogen into groundwater and nearby streams. In central New England openings formed when hemlocks have died from the woolly adelgid are often filled by black birch. The shift from a long-lived conifer casting year-round shade with slowly decomposing needles to a shorter-lived, deciduous species with rapidly decomposing leaves can trigger a cascading set of changes in nutrient cycling. Researchers have studied the effects of loss of hemlocks on animal species ranging from spiders to butterflies to birds and small mammals. A lot of work has focused on the distinctive effects of hemlocks along headwater streams, where the deep shade can help prevent high water temperatures in the summer that can threaten trout.

There is little question that a dense grove of hemlocks creates a distinctive environment and associated community of species. Many of these effects are identifiable even at the neighborhood scale around individual scattered hemlocks in a more diverse stand. I have two concerns, however, with the emphasis on hemlock (or any other tree) as a foundation species. The first is largely academic. Very few of the studies purporting to demonstrate the uniqueness of eastern hemlock have done a rigorous comparison with other species in northeastern forests. And I'm pretty certain that a long list of distinctive features would be cataloged if the same amount of effort was devoted to studying any other northeastern tree species that is at least locally abundant. There is a corollary to Gleason's individualistic principle at work here. Just as tree species are distributed individualistically along environmental gradients, without clustering into clearly defined community types, every one of our tree species has a unique set of ecological traits and impacts on ecosystem function. There is certainly overlap and functional redundancy among species along some of these axes, but I see no objective basis for elevating any particular tree species to foundation status.

That leads to my second and more philosophical concern. Many of the studies focused on designating eastern hemlock as a foundation species were explicit that this justified elevating the concern about the loss of that particular species due to the woolly adelgid. That at least implies that there is less reason to be alarmed by the loss of tree species that don't achieve status as foundational. I find that unacceptable both intellectually and ethically. The emerald ash borer threatens decimation or worse for presumably the entire list of ash species in eastern North America as well as the rarer ash species found in the western United States. Only one of those, the swamp species black ash, would likely rate as a foundation species, since the upland ash species are typically well mixed in forests with other species. There is little doubt that elimination of black ash from swamps where it is dominant can thoroughly transform those wetlands. There is indeed evidence that those forested swamps can convert to open marshes when the black ash die rather than be replaced by other species of wetland trees.[7] But there is currently little reason to expect such dramatic ecological effects of the decimation of the three more widespread species of upland ashes, white ash, green ash, and blue ash. Does this mean we need to focus only on preventing the loss of black ash from swamps where it is common in the upper Midwest?

The trap of utilitarianism as a justification for action is even more apparent when you couch the issue in terms of measurable economic costs. There is always a bit of back-of-the-envelope reckoning in the predictions of the economic costs of any one forest pest or pathogen. Despite the guesswork inherent in those calculations, it seems clear that by far the greatest costs are associated with the loss of street and yard trees rather than the death of trees in working forests. It can cost thousands of dollars for an arborist to safely remove a single dead or dying tree in a yard or along a street. And the loss of tree cover has well-documented impacts on human well-being and property values. Only the highest quality sawlogs harvested from a working forest could compete with those values. Eastern hemlock and white ash, two species currently threatened with decimation, have some of the lowest timber value among northeastern conifers and hardwoods, respectively. Both hemlock and white ash are popular in yards, and white ash was widely planted along city streets as a replacement for elms felled by Dutch elm disease. Chemical methods are available to homeowners and municipal arborists to protect individual hemlocks and white ash from their pests, but the costs would be prohibitive for any meaningful acreage of forests. Does this mean we should write off the losses of hemlock and white ash in working forests and just focus on saving them in yards and along streets?

My answer is an emphatic no, and I don't know anyone who has argued otherwise. This may seem a bit naïve but is heartfelt nonetheless. If pushed to justify the position that we should not give up on any of our tree species I would probably fall back on the precautionary principle and note that we rarely possess enough information during the early stages of a new infestation to accurately predict the cascade of long-term ecological, economic, and social consequences of the decimation of yet another native tree species.

But the ethical imperative to fight these battles is far more compelling to me. That said, resources are clearly limited, and tactics matter. We need to be able to rapidly address the nature of the threat once a new pest or pathogen is discovered and allocate resources in ways that have the best chance of minimizing the extent of the loss. And those resources are both financial and human. Twenty years ago I wasn't sure enough new graduate students were being trained with the necessary expertise that blended forest entomology and pathology with an ecological perspective. Today, I see a much stronger investment in that much-needed human capital. Funding is always tight, but that's nothing new.

One of the most common questions I encounter about the threat from introduced pests and pathogens is whether the problem will only get worse under climate change. The simple answer is almost certainly yes but with important caveats. With the exception of the hemlock woolly adelgid, each of the members of the rogue's gallery in table 1 has climatic range limits that already encompass the entire range of the tree species it attacks; thus it doesn't require a change in climate to blanket the current distribution of its new host. Various studies have documented almost complete mortality in hemlock woolly adelgids exposed to extremely cold temperatures (far below 0° F.), and minimum winter temperatures appear to explain the current northern range limit of hemlock mortality from the adelgid across central New England. Over the past twenty years adelgid populations have repeatedly built up on hemlocks in the Cary Institute woods only to be killed back in years with extremely cold winters before the adelgid levels could reach concentrations that would kill most of our hemlocks. Unfortunately, our climate monitoring station shows that the most pronounced change in our weather has been an increase in winter temperatures. Even the most optimistic of the scenarios coming out of climate change research imply that the refugium provided to northern hemlocks by cold winters will shrink dramatically in coming decades. There is also evidence that the adelgids are evolving greater cold tolerance as they move northward.[8]

More generally, some of the pests and pathogens listed in table 1 are more likely to attack and kill trees that are already stressed by some other factor in their environment. And it is certainly reasonable to assume that climate change will be one of those stresses. But almost all of the pests and pathogens listed in table 1 are capable of eventually killing infested trees. Other stresses, including climate, typically influence just how quickly, not whether, the tree succumbs. Gypsy moth defoliation and insect defoliators in general are the obvious exception. Widespread defoliation inspires lots of public concern, often with calls for widespread applications of insecticides. Most trees, however, produce new leaves within a matter of weeks, and outright mortality is typically limited to otherwise stressed trees. Indeed, some native insects, like the forest tent caterpillars, periodically build up massive populations that can defoliate trees across large regions but usually without lasting impacts on tree population dynamics. At the height of the massive gypsy moth outbreak in central and southern New England in late June 1980 and 1981, the caterpillars consumed almost all of the foliage of all tree species in forests across the region. We examined impacts of the defoliation in forests at the Cary Institute and found dramatic declines in tree growth the next year or two but very little outright mortality except among heavily shaded understory and subcanopy hemlocks.[9] Producing hemlock needles is a significant investment that the tree recoups because the needles remain photosynthetically active for at least several years. Canopy hemlock trees appear to have had sufficient energy reserves to refoliate after the defoliation and suffered very little mortality. But we lost large numbers of the understory hemlocks, and I have always assumed that defoliation depleted their carbohydrate reserves to a point that they could not recover next year. This loss might not seem like a notable event, given all of the other currents swirling around our oak forests. But those understory and subcanopy hemlocks had been positioned to eventually replace the overstory oaks. It was a vivid demonstration of the ability of a single insect outbreak to redirect the course of forest succession.

As an aside, each of our native tree species is host to dozens of native pests and pathogens. Localized outbreaks of those insects and diseases are common, although it is usually only the really extensive outbreaks like the forest tent caterpillars and spruce budworm that get noticed by the public. But we have very little handle on whether the frequency and intensity of those outbreaks are increasing or decreasing and, in either case, whether this might be linked to climate change, air pollution, or any other changes in the environment. The threats from introduced pests and pathogens are clear and present even in the absence of any other stressors. So, somewhat counterintuitively, I suspect that we should be more concerned about whether climate change could alter the currently benign balance between our tree species and their natural pathogens and insect consumers.

Each year brings the discovery of yet a new threat from an introduced forest pest or pathogen. A dozen new wood-boring insects have been detected in the United States each decade for the past thirty years, with enormous economic and ecological impacts.[10] Estimates of the total costs of the emerald ash borer by the year 2020 exceed $12 billion. The bulk of these costs are borne by local governments and individual homeowners in costs for tree removal and replacement and lost property values. Given that international trade, either in live plants or the use of solid wood packing materials, is the source of almost all of these introductions, the first line of defense obviously rests in international trade policies. US plant import regulations date back almost a century and have been swamped by the explosive growth in live-plant imports over the past thirty years. There have been some promising developments in those regulations in the past decade, notably the development of a list of live plants that are not approved for import pending a pest risk analysis. There is a fairly complicated process both for adding plants to the list and for conducting the risk analysis needed before the new plant species can be removed from the quarantine list. The process is new enough that its effectiveness is uncertain (at least to me). One challenge is that for a plant to be added to the list it has to be a known host of a known pest. This leaves us vulnerable to unknown pests on new hosts. I would be surprised if anyone was willing to argue that even with this new program existing international trade regulations are sufficient to meaningfully slow the pace of introductions.

Led by Gary Lovett at the Cary Institute and coauthors from ten other institutions, a study of the impacts and policy options for introduced forest insects and diseases in the United States outlines a number of new trade policies that could help stem the tide. Their peer-reviewed paper was published in a prominent scientific journal. This is a necessary first step in establishing credibility but is usually also the point at which scientists back off and hope, vainly in most cases, that regulators and legislators take notice. There are many good reasons why scientists tend to shy away from policy debates, and even stronger professional disincentives and barriers to getting involved. But I think there was consensus among the authors of the study that there was an even greater imperative to reach a broader audience. The result is an integrated set of proposed new policies and practices called Tree-SMART Trade. The proposal outlines new efforts in five concrete areas: switching to pest-free packing materials for international shipments; minimizing new outbreaks with better early detection and rapid response; augmenting pest prevention programs with international trade partners; restricting the importation of live plants in the same genera as native woody plants; and tightening enforcement of penalties.[11]

The specific proposals in Tree-SMART Trade all seem eminently sensible to me, and I am confident that any objective analysis would show far greater economic benefits than costs.

But as is true of so many environmental issues, the costs and benefits of solutions don't all accrue to the same groups, and I don't think Lovett and his colleagues are at all naïve about the challenges they face in advancing their proposals. That just makes me all the more heartened by their willingness to step outside of their traditional roles as scientists.[12]

One of the areas outlined in Tree-SMART Trade addresses the second line of defense, namely, the rapid detection of new forest pests and pathogens that get past import controls. While the US Department of Agriculture shoulders most of this burden, through APHIS and the Forest Service, responsibility is dispersed across many other federal, state, and local agencies as well as forest industry and conservation groups. And it is fair to say that, through education and media campaigns, all of these levels work to recruit the public as sentinels. As in the case of the broader efforts to control invasive species in general, there seems little question that early detection is critical, even if it is only to get a head start on research to develop eventual control measures.

To date, the most successful effort to control an initial infestation has been that concerned with the Asian longhorned beetle. The control measures are simple but brutal. Rapid and thorough surveys of potential host trees within a mile or more around any infested tree are conducted, and any trees with signs of the presence of the beetle are cut down and destroyed. This can devastate a neighborhood if it loses all of its street and shade trees, but the beetles threaten such a broad range of eastern tree species that there is currently no viable alternative. A number of outbreaks, particularly one in and around Chicago, have been eradicated, and there is reason to hope that the beetle can be controlled and soon eradicated in the remaining active infestations in the greater New York City region, southwestern Ohio, and Worcester, Massachusetts. But there are no guarantees that new infestations won't be discovered.

The success of the control efforts for the Asian longhorned beetle is one of the few bright spots in this story and owes at least part of its success to the low fecundity and slow rates of dispersal of the insect. The emerald ash borer is a case in point. APHIS was just as aggressive in the initial efforts to control that insect when it was discovered in the Midwest, but the ash borer had already established numerous satellite infestations by the time it was discovered in 2002. Inadvertent dispersal by humans via infested firewood, logs, and nursery stock, for example, was likely most to blame, but that, combined with the difficulty of identifying the early stages of an infestation at a new site and the high reproductive rate and active flight of the insect, appears to have overwhelmed local control efforts. A study has shown that the ash borer had the highest average rate of spread, fifty-seven kilometers per year, of any of the seven introduced insects and six diseases analyzed.[13]

Our poor track record of containing initial infestations is disheartening. And while that record doesn't reduce the imperative to get better at detection and early control of new pests and pathogens, it does mean that in most cases we are faced with trying to slow their spread while searching for control methods that can work over large areas. In most cases that means finding some combination of biological or chemical control, hopefully in the broader context of integrated pest management. Both of these come with substantial risks of their own. A typical approach for biological control is to search for natural predators, parasitoids, or pathogens from the native range, that is, overseas, of an insect pest and then screen them to see if they can be safely introduced to effectively control the pest in its new range. The concerns here are obvious, above all the risk that the introduced control agent might attack native insects or otherwise wreak havoc with the native food web. Biological control has a very checkered past and is often highlighted in textbooks as a classic example of the risks of tinkering with nature. But chemical control through widespread pesticide use can be just as risky and typically feasible only on individual street and yard trees.

Unfortunately, other than in the case of the Asian longhorned beetle I can't yet point to successful methods of controlling any of the pests and pathogens listed in table 1 in a forest setting. But I do see lots of good science being done by more and more researchers around the country to find solutions, despite the fact that funding is, if anything, getting tighter. Luckily there is strong public interest, and some research groups have turned to crowdsourcing the funds they need. Avenues being explored run the gamut from a long list of potential biological control agents to genetically engineering resistance to such diseases as chestnut blight to rapid selection and breeding of resistant genotypes of ashes. One of the most intriguing is the possibility that a nonlethal, or hypovirulent, strain of the chestnut blight fungus could be coaxed into spreading and outcompeting the virulent form (fig. 18). As a vital but last resort botanical gardens and other groups are creating tree seed archives so that we can preserve genetic diversity for a future where we have effective controls.[14]

I cannot say I am confident that we can slow the rate of arrival of new pests and pathogens and eventually find controls to allow the victims of past introductions to begin to recover. But I am at least hopeful we can begin to stem the tide. For most of the species that have already been decimated, the "seeds" of recovery are still in the woods, in the form of widely scattered seedlings, saplings, and the occasional adult tree. In principle,

Figure 18. The distinctive leaves of an American chestnut (*Castanea dentata*). Once one of the most majestic trees of eastern forests, it now persists as saplings and small trees in which the trunk eventually becomes infected with chestnut blight, dies back to the root system, and then resprouts. Photo by author.

once control measures are found, those species can begin to rebuild their populations. As a forest ecologist I am used to thinking on the timescales of generations of trees: hundreds of years, not decades. It seems inevitable that any recovery will be measured in centuries at best, even if actively supplemented with propagation and planting schemes. So the more immediate question is which of our native tree species will be decimated by the next pest or pathogen that reaches our shores?

11

Storm Clouds Looming

Introduced pests and pathogens have been wreaking havoc with northeastern forests for over a century, and new ones are likely to continue to do so, at least until we see major changes in international trade policies. There is little question, however, that climate change represents the greatest environmental threat on the horizon for humans and natural ecosystems worldwide. Not all ecosystems will be equally sensitive to climate change, and my research over the past ten years leads me to the inescapable conclusion that even fairly extreme climate change scenarios will have little immediate impact on the distribution and abundance of tree species in northeastern forests. My recently published empirical foundation for this conclusion is based on an analysis of the climate sensitivities of the recruitment, growth, and survival of the fifty most common tree species in eastern North America.[1] The bottom line is that the growth and survival of both saplings and canopy trees of almost all of the species are sufficiently insensitive to variation in either temperature or precipitation that displacement by more southerly species generally takes two hundred to three hundred years, that is, two to three generations, even without any limitations in the rates of northward dispersal of tree seeds. The notable exceptions are for several species of northern conifers such as balsam fir and white spruce. The computer models that colleagues and I have developed predict that those species will begin to decline precipitously in our region within the next fifty years, in large part because adults of those species show high mortality rates at the southern edges of their current ranges.

Tree seedlings, on the other hand, are much more sensitive to variation in climate and, by extension, to climate change. This is not unexpected since small seedlings are more vulnerable than even small saplings to all sorts of stresses. Thus after several centuries, when the current generations of saplings and adults have died out, the expected changes in the composition of our forests will indeed be profound, including both significant northward range shifts for many species and the formation of novel species assemblages. The nature of those new forests will reflect not only the direct impacts of climate change but also the myriad interactions between climate change and all of the other human influences discussed in this book. For example, our analyses suggest that oaks and hickories will not simply move northward to displace species like sugar maple and beech. Instead, under the combined effects of continued fire suppression, high deer densities, and selective logging, our analyses predict that with the exception of northern red oak the remaining oaks and the hickories will show long-term declines in northeastern forests. The winners instead are species like white pine and tulip poplar, both of which benefit from warmer temperatures and show adequate regeneration under partial harvesting and current deer densities.

There are many lines of evidence supporting the hypothesis that the temperate forests of eastern North America may be slow to respond to climate change. But there are also real limits to my confidence in predictions of how eastern forests

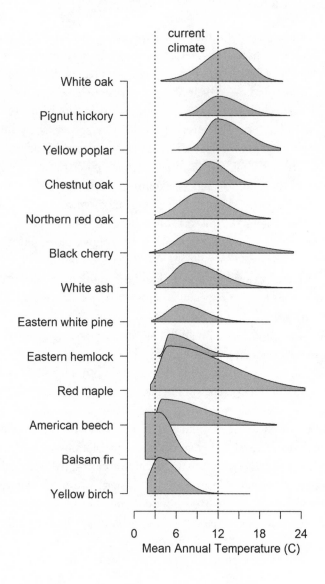

current
climate

White oak

Pignut hickory

Yellow poplar

Chestnut oak

Northern red oak

Black cherry

White ash

Eastern white pine

Eastern hemlock

Red maple

American beech

Balsam fir

Yellow birch

0   6   12   18   24
Mean Annual Temperature (C)

will respond to climate change. So it is worth stepping back to consider the evolution and biogeography of our tree species to put this issue in context. One of the most distinctive features of the moist, temperate forests of the northern hemisphere (eastern North America, western Europe, and temperate regions of Asia) is a steady decline from south to north in tree species diversity. The gradient is most pronounced in the broad-leaved species (Angiosperms) rather than the conifers (Gymnosperms). While conifers are the dominant species in forests in the coldest climates of the northern hemisphere, only a relatively small fraction of the species in the world's families and genera of broad-leaved trees have evolved the traits necessary for tolerance of cold climates, thereby enabling them to radiate outward from the tropics. The farther north you go, the fewer lineages of broad-leaved trees there are that can tolerate the increasingly extreme fluctuations between summer and winter weather.

But the upshot is that one of the most distinctive features of northeastern tree species is their ability to tolerate, at least as adults, enormous variation in temperature and on timescales as short as day to day. With few exceptions all of the northeastern tree species can be found across a very wide range of mean annual temperature (fig. 19). Within those ranges the fraction

---

Figure 19. Frequency of occurrence of thirteen common tree species in northeastern US forests, as a function of mean annual temperature (°C). The curves were fitted using data from the approximately 160,000 Forest Inventory and Analysis plots in upland forests of the thirty-one eastern states. The curves show the percentage of plots at a given temperature that contain a species. The curves are scaled so that the vertical spacing between the horizontal baselines for the species represents a frequency of 50 percent. The current range of mean annual temperature (calculated during the years from 2000 to 2015) for the nine northeastern states ranges from approximately 3°C to 12°C.

of stands within which a species occurs varies widely, with a clear peak at some presumably optimal temperature. As you go north or south of that peak, you'll find that species in fewer and fewer stands. Species of cold climates tend to have peak frequencies near their low temperature range limits, with "long tails" to warmer climates. Just the opposite is true of species with peak frequencies in warmer climates (see fig. 19). There is far less variation across the range of a species in its relative abundance if you do find it in a stand. So a species that is typically abundant when found at the southern edge of its range is typically just as abundant, on average, when found at the northern end of its range. There are a number of possible explanations for these patterns, but they are at least consistent with the hypothesis that seedling establishment is the critical life history stage and that once a species gets established within a stand factors other than climate determine how locally abundant it will be.[2]

There seems little question that the patterns in figure 19 are more than just correlation and that climate, particularly temperature, has indeed played an important role in the historical distributions of our tree species. It has proven much more difficult to determine exactly what aspect of climate is important for the distribution of any given tree species. It is often assumed that the northern range limits are set by tolerance of extremely low winter temperatures, but determining exactly how cold, how frequent, or how long those cold spells need to be turns out to be an almost intractable problem for statistical reasons. Not the least of the challenges is that there are so many permutations of temperature data to consider, and they are all correlated among themselves to some degree. In contrast, southern range limits are often assumed to reflect displacement by competition with species better adapted to warmer conditions rather than an inability of the northern species to tolerate warmer climates. As intuitively appealing as this hypothesis is, it too has proven to be difficult to test.

With the exception of the range limits along the prairie–forest border in the Midwest, distributions of eastern tree species don't show nearly such consistent variation along gradients of total annual rainfall. This may simply be due to the fact that average annual rainfall is not a very biologically meaningful aspect of climate. Nor is it a very good proxy for more biologically relevant measures of soil moisture availability or drought stress during the growing season. The amount of soil moisture available to a tree is the product of the combined effects of rainfall, temperature, humidity, net solar radiation as affected by latitude, slope, and aspect, and soil water-holding capacity. Thus an area with any given total annual rainfall can have a great deal of site-to-site variation in soil moisture regimes. It is clear that eastern tree species differ markedly in their responses to soil moisture supply and their tolerance of drought. But given the wide range of soil moisture regimes present just along a slope from a ridgetop to a valley bottom, regional variation in rainfall is only weakly related to the geographic distributions of most eastern tree species. The distribution of beech in eastern North America is perhaps the most striking exception. In the upper Midwest the western range limit for beech hugs the western shore of Lake Michigan in Wisconsin and extends northward into the eastern half of the Upper Peninsula of Michigan. The current western range boundary for beech has been relatively stable for much of the past eight thousand years, but scattered outlier populations can be found in the modern landscape.[3] The long-term average temperatures and rainfall where it is absent in the rest of Wisconsin and the western portions of the Upper Peninsula are broadly similar to the lower peninsula of Michigan, where beech is abundant. But the upper Midwest has a much more continental climate than the northeastern states, and there is evidence that the western portions of the region experience more severe droughts than the northeast. And beech is one of the most drought sensitive of the northeastern tree species. So I suspect that this is a case in which infrequent but extreme droughts rather than long-term average rainfall patterns set at least one portion of the range boundary of one of our tree species.

Ecologists have used a number of approaches to predict how tree species distributions will respond to climate change. The most direct approach uses statistical correlations to relate the current geographic distribution of species to climate variables and then applies those correlations to map species onto whatever future climates are projected for a region. These so-called species distribution models have a strong empirical foundation because of the wealth of both forest inventory and climate data. But their use in projecting future distributions of tree species under climate change is based on a number of highly problematic assumptions. Most notable is the assumption that the geographic distributions of species can keep pace with rapid changes in climate. I consider this assumption dubious even for the very modest rates of natural fluctuations in climate observed at various times during the past twelve thousand years. Estimates of the potential rates of migration of northeastern tree species vary widely, but a consensus is emerging that the rates are generally far lower than would be necessary for most tree species to stay in equilibrium with even past rates of variation in climate, let alone the rapid rates of climate change that will occur in the near future. The models also assume that the range limits of tree species are set primarily by physical factors (climate) rather than by biotic interactions. This conflicts with the widely held assumption that while the northern limits of temperate tree species may be set by physical limitations of climate, the southern limits are more often set by competition with species adapted to warmer climates. Because of these limitations the models are best viewed as a tool for projections of changes in potential suitable habitat for a species or ecosystem under a changing climate. My sense is that there is close to consensus among forest ecologists that those models vastly overestimate the pace of future shifts in tree species distributions under climate change.

A very different class of models tries to predict changes in the distributions of entire biomes and ecosystem types, for example, boreal forest versus temperate forest versus grassland. These models use much more mechanistic relationships between climate and processes like biogeochemistry and plant physiology. But those models typically group species into very broadly defined functional types of plants like warm season grasses, cool season grasses, shrubs, broad-leaved trees, and conifers. Similar to the species distribution models, these process models can predict very rapid shifts in the boundaries between different biomes. But like the species distribution models they generally don't take into account processes that would limit actual rates of plant migration, and they provide little detail about shifts in species distributions within broadly defined biomes such as the eastern temperate forest.

The third general approach has been based on demography, in which the effects of climate change are incorporated in models that focus on the underlying processes of reproduction, seed dispersal, seedling establishment, and the subsequent growth and survival of saplings and adult trees. As I've mentioned elsewhere, this is the approach I have favored for many reasons, not the least of which is that to my mind it comes closest to balancing a sufficient level of mechanistic realism with the availability of the necessary field data (drawing heavily from the forest inventory data network). Perhaps more important, this approach makes it possible to place climate change in the context of the many other currents shaping the future of our forests. There are many models in this genre in use by research groups around the world, and they all differ from each other in various ways. I have to admit that when our first analyses in 2011 told us not to expect major shifts in the distribution or abundance of tree species for at least two hundred years, even under fairly extreme climate change scenarios, we went back to the data and the model to see what we could have missed. We now have access to even more data and have refined our analyses of how climate affects many disparate aspects of tree demography, but the basic model predictions have not changed. And I have been heartened to see that other models, developed independently by other research groups, have come to the same general conclusions.[4] The broad patterns of forest succession triggered by past land use history, combined with the pervasive but highly selective effects of timber harvesting and the decimation of individual species by pests and pathogens, swamp likely climate change effects in northeastern forests for at least the next two hundred years (fig. 20). Our analyses, if anything, overestimate the potential for range shifts, since we assume that once the climate becomes suitable for seedling establishment some seedlings will manage to find their way to the site. While the new arrivals may have a competitive advantage in the new climate, the current canopy trees still provide a numerical advantage for continued regeneration from the abundant local seed rain they provide. And there is currently little evidence to suggest that warmer climates in the Northeast will shorten the expected life spans of the current canopy trees.

So, while I expect northeastern forests to drift for several generations, there are definitely rapids ahead. And there are many reasons why it is difficult to know just how dangerous those rapids are. All models are simplifications, by both necessity and design. My philosophy has been to minimize the number of free parameters in our model—involving processes that we think might be important but for which we can only guess at certain key parameters. There is active research on many of these processes and reason to expect that the models can be constantly refined. But as I admitted at the outset of this chapter there are many sources of uncertainty in our current predictions of forest response to climate change, and it's worth reviewing them briefly here.

Trees may be firmly rooted, but their seeds and their genes, via pollen, can potentially travel great distances. Paleoecologists have debated for years whether the northward rates of migration of tree species following retreat of the glaciers were limited by seed dispersal or whether there was sufficient, if rare, long-distance dispersal so that species could keep pace with natural fluctuations in climate over the past twelve thousand years. I don't expect a definitive answer to that fundamentally historical question, but we now know a great deal more about the effective dispersal distances for tree seeds than we did when paleoecologists first raised the issue that dispersal limitation could be important to the postglacial record. The question has far more salience today, given the rapid rates of climate change expected during this century. Seed weights of northeastern tree species span almost six orders of magnitude, from fewer than one hundred seeds per kilogram in black walnut to over six million per kilogram in the aspens. The minuscule seeds of the aspens and birches are the champions when it comes to prolific long-distance dispersal by wind. It's not a coincidence that these species are

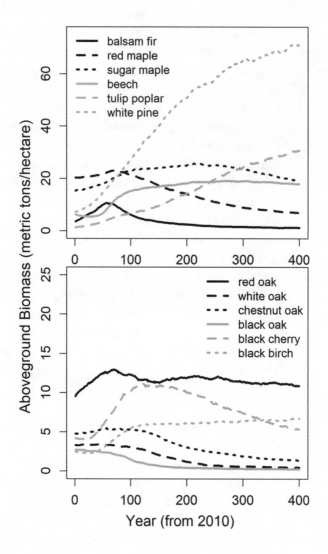

Figure 20. Predicted changes in average aboveground biomass over the next four hundred years for six common tree species in northern forests (*top*) and six common species of southern forests (*bottom*), within the nine northeastern states (Pennsylvania and New Jersey north). The predictions were generated using a forest simulation model (SORTIE-ND), including the effects of the current forest harvest regime, current levels of air pollution via nitrogen deposition, the projected spread of the trees' major current pests and pathogens in the region (beech bark disease, emerald ash borer, and the hemlock woolly adelgid), and a climate change scenario in which mean annual temperature increases by 3°C and precipitation increases 15 percent over the next one hundred years, then plateaus. Changes in species abundance for the first two hundred years are primarily due to successional dynamics given past land use history and the effects of the selective logging regimes. Not shown are the rapid declines in abundance of white ash due to the emerald ash borer during the next thirty years, and the rapid decline in eastern hemlock abundance in the next fifty to sixty years as warmer winters allow the northward spread of the hemlock wooly adelgid. Balsam fir is projected to increase for the next fifty years because of highly successful regeneration in low-elevation northern forests under partial harvesting but then begin to decline precipitously as a result of climate change. Northern red oak maintains roughly its current average abundance throughout the period, but the other major oak species are all projected to show significant declines even under a warming climate, largely due to competition from the two species—white pine and tulip poplar—that are the main beneficiaries of warmer climates in this region. The average aboveground biomass of forests in the nine-state region is predicted to rise from its current average of 114 metric tons per hectare to 162 metric tons per hectare in 2110, and 193 metric tons per hectare by 2410. Much of that rise can be attributed to the dramatic rise in biomass of white pine and tulip poplar. The details of the simulation methods are provided in Michelle L. Brown, Charles D. Canham, Lora Murphy, and Therese M. Donovan, "Timber Harvest as the Predominant Disturbance Regime in Northeastern U.S. Forests: Effects of Harvest Intensification," *Ecosphere* 9 (2018): e02062. 10.1002/ecs2.2062.

mostly pioneers, in which ability to disperse widely to colonize recent disturbances is an essential trait. Many of our conifers also have very small seeds with modest wings that allow reasonable long-distance dispersal. The maples and ashes have moderate to large seeds but with correspondingly large wings to facilitate wind dispersal. The mean dispersal distances for those species are typically only tens of meters, although some of their seeds can travel extraordinary distances when swept away by strong winds and updrafts in storms. Our largest-seeded tree species, the oaks, hickories, and walnuts, are all voraciously consumed by birds and small mammals. Some of the seeds that are carried away and hidden for consumption later in the winter inevitably escape. There are surprisingly few studies of just how far birds and, to a lesser degree, mammals move these large seeds, but my sense is that the distances are rarely greater than a kilometer.

Given this enormous variation in dispersal ability it seems likely that rates of northward migration during the coming century will vary dramatically among tree species, with dispersal ability a potential limitation in all but the smallest-seeded species. In addition, we should remember that the natural rates of mortality of seedlings and saplings are high and that reaching reproductive size within a forest setting typically takes a score of years or longer. So the odds that any single seed dispersed from afar can reach maturity and establish a new population are exceedingly small, particularly in competition with the large numbers of seeds produced by the local canopy trees. As a result, it's hard to imagine northward migration of tree species as anything other than the chance establishment of new satellite populations beyond a species' current range, with far more gradual backfilling behind those outliers.[5]

The ability of saplings and adults of most of our tree species to tolerate a warmer and particularly wetter climate with little increase in rates of mortality is at the heart of current predictions of their delayed responses to climate change. Dispersal limitation would simply lead to even longer time lags between climate change and shifts in species distribution and abundance. But those expectations could change dramatically if evidence emerges to challenge the notion that resident trees can persist until eventually being replaced by new generations of seedlings that are more competitive in the new climate. At least three issues come to mind. The first flows from growing evidence of changes in the seasonal phenology of trees. One of the most readily documented effects of climate change on plants has been a shift to earlier bud break in the spring and, to a lesser extent, later leaf senescence in the fall. At first glance a longer growing season would seem to benefit most plants. But somewhat counterintuitively there is mounting evidence that earlier bud break is exposing the newly forming leaves of many species to greater risk of late spring frost damage.[6] I'm not yet convinced this stress is substantial enough to change the basic story of the tolerance of current saplings and adults to warmer climates, but it is just one example of the potential mismatch we can expect in the complex ways climate serves as a signal for the timing of all sorts of critical biological activities, not just in plants but all species.

The second issue I lose sleep over is a corollary of this mismatch in phenology, but in this case due to the potential for changes in climate to alter the balance between tree species and their native pests and pathogens. I've already argued that introduced pests and pathogens are a dire threat even in the absence of climate change. But each of our native tree species has a whole host of native insects and diseases that are typically only secondary agents of tree mortality; they serve as the proximate cause of death of an otherwise stressed or damaged tree. The life histories of many of these native pests and pathogens are sensitive to climate, and there is mounting evidence, at least in western forests, that climate change is altering the virulence of some native pathogens and the magnitude and severity of native pest outbreaks. The best-studied examples come from the outbreaks of mountain pine beetle (*Dendroctonus ponderosae*) and dothistroma needle blight, a fungal disease caused by *Dothistroma septosporum*. Both have caused widespread defoliation and death, especially of lodgepole pines, in western forests. The bark beetles appear to be benefiting from warmer weather, while the outbreaks of needle blight in British Columbia appear to be due to wetter summers.[7] The interior Rocky Mountain region has seen more striking increases in mean annual temperatures than the Northeast in the past two decades, and I can't yet point to comparable threats to northeastern trees from native pests or pathogens. But the threat remains very real.

The third issue that could change the basic story of the delayed responses of forests to climate change involves direct human intervention to, somewhat paradoxically, speed up the response via preemptive logging and/or implementation of what's called assisted migration, the deliberate planting of southern species well north of their current distributions. Preemptive logging is already taking place to preferentially harvest species like white ash that are threatened by introduced pests and pathogens. I have not yet seen evidence of preferential harvesting of species near their southern range limits in anticipation that those species would be most at risk of reduced growth and increased mortality under climate change. But this is certainly a subject being discussed in the context of future forest management. The topic of assisted migration has generated controversy within the conservation biology community, given the somewhat obvious concerns raised by the deliberate

introduction of any organism into a new habitat or outside its
(current) native range. The issue is less controversial in forest
management, particularly in plantation forestry, where there is
a long history of studies to determine the best seed sources to
use in establishing new plantations in a given location. It seems
eminently sensible to consider future climates in making those
decisions. But plantation forestry is rare in the northeastern
United States, and I have a hard time imagining the circum-
stances that would justify the efforts of a modern-day Johnny
Appleseed spreading seeds or planting seedlings of southern
tree species in northeastern forests.

There is at least one other wild card in predicting responses of tree species (or any other organisms) to climate
change. That is the potential for either genetic adaptation
within a local population or the phenotypic acclimation of
individuals to a changing environment. Most of the analyses I
and others have done to assess how tree species will respond to
a new climate suffer from a basic limitation: we compare the
performance of a species in one portion of its range to the
performance of the species in parts of its range with a different
climate. The implicit assumption is that, for example, trees in a
colder climate will behave like the trees from warmer climates
once the cold climate warms. This is known within the business
as a space-for-time substitution. To date there have been few
viable alternatives to this approach. The obvious improvement
is to use long-term studies at a wide range of sites and track
variation in demography as a function of year-to-year variation
in climate at each location. In fact, the change in design of the
US Forest Service forest inventory network implemented in
1999 means that soon there will be enough remeasurements at
each of the several hundred thousand forest inventory plots in
the eastern United States to do exactly this. But in the meantime

there is one other obvious alternative—at least for reconstructing how tree growth has responded to variation in past
climates—and that is through the analysis of tree rings. Den-
droecologists have been perfecting methods for analysis of tree
rings for decades. Aside from the obvious interest in understanding controls on tree growth, tree rings have been used to
address questions ranging from the climatic conditions that
create the perfect sounding board for a Stradivarius violin to
the dating of timbers in archeological digs to reconstructing
the historical frequencies of earthquakes.

Analyses of tree cores collected from sites with diverse
climate histories can tell you if trees from different portions of
the range of a species show fundamentally dissimilar responses to year-to-year variation in climate. The null hypothesis
(implicit in the space-for-time substitution studies) is that trees
throughout the range of a species have the same underlying
response to variation in climate. Colleagues and I recently
completed an analysis of over twenty-three thousand tree cores
collected by the US Forest Service from forest inventory plots
across the region from Ohio to Maine.[8] There were adequate
samples for fourteen tree species, and in all fourteen there was
evidence of either phenotypic acclimation or genetic adaptation
to the long-term average climate at individual locations, rather
than simply response to the absolute value of either temperature
or precipitation. In most of the species growth was highest in
years that were cooler and wetter than the long-term average
at the site, regardless of whether the site was at the warm or
cold or wet or dry portion of the range of the species.

The analyses don't allow us to distinguish between true
genetic adaptations within the local populations versus the
simpler acclimation of individuals phenotypically; for instance,
by using cues from the local environment to build a root system

that optimizes growth in the cool, wet years that have high soil moisture availability and little drought stress. If the results are genetically based, we need to know how quickly these species can adapt to a far more rapidly changing climate than they have experienced at any time in millennia. This at least raises the possibility that the species could be even more sensitive to rapid climate change than indicated by the space-for-time substitution studies. But if the results are phenotypic and reflect physiological or morphological acclimation that a tree develops during its life span, this potential to acclimate to local climate could help buffer species in the face of climate change. The bottom line is that we need to know much more about the nature both of genetic differentiation within the ranges of these broadly distributed tree species and of their potential to acclimate physiologically and morphologically to changing climates.

Finally, the real wild card in all of this is that we still don't know just how severe climate change will be. This is in large part because there is so much uncertainty about the future of greenhouse gas emissions. That the earth's climate will warm significantly over the next fifty to one hundred years as a result of human activity appears inevitable. The question is by how much and how quickly and whether it can be contained before reaching catastrophic levels. But there is the added uncertainty in downscaling predictions from the global climate change models to predictions at regional scales. This is particularly true for downscaled predictions of regional changes in the amounts and seasonal distribution of rainfall; most of the climate change models predict slightly wetter weather for the Northeast, but there is much less certainty about this than about changes in temperatures. And the models are even more uncertain in their ability to predict the frequency and severity of extreme weather events like droughts, heat waves, and hurricanes. There are

reasons to believe that eastern forests in general and northeastern forests in particular are more resilient in the face of such
events than many other ecosystems in the United States, but
the fact remains that when it comes to climate change, we are
entering truly uncharted waters.

12

What Lies Ahead?

If I had to trace my preoccupation with forest dynamics back to a single event, it would be to a walk I took in the woods of the Hudson Highlands as a teenager. Wandering beneath a canopy of towering oaks and armed only with a woody plant field guide, I noticed that one of the trees was growing out of the old stone foundation of a long-gone farmhouse. What I had naively assumed to be the tranquility of an ancient forest hid a deep, complex history. I still find tranquility in any walk in the woods, but forty years of research have made me much more alert to both where that forest has been and where it is headed.

The reestablishment of northeastern forests over the past century has restored many of the ecological, economic, and social benefits that forests provide. But it also represents the emergence of a landscape with no historical precedent. I have not been able to entirely let go of the emotional tug of the primeval and have no intention of forsaking the appeal of wilderness, but I am no longer able to walk in any forest without recognizing that humans have shaped and will continue to shape what I see.

The ability to decipher at least the recent history of a forest doesn't require much more than paying attention while walking, and there are many guides to the clues that will allow you to read the history of the landscape along the way.[1] Peering ahead is more difficult. The various computer models that forest ecologists have developed can be used to project the logical consequences of any given future scenario, at least in the context of the mechanisms captured in the model. But there is so much uncertainty about the future of the many external forces affecting our forests that I rarely think of the output from those models as predictions, let alone concrete forecasts. But the models provide one of our best tools to integrate the many currents at work and can at least point to where those currents would logically lead.

In the simple metrics of forest cover and biomass, the successional dynamics triggered by human land use over the past several centuries provide some reassuring trends. The wave of human activity that has had the most pervasive impact on northeastern forests—the clearing of almost three-quarters of the Northeast's forests and subsequent regrowth—has passed us by. In its wake there are only ripples, and it's hard for me to see any meaningful changes in total forest cover on the immediate horizon. But then again, no one seems to be able to forecast the truly transformational economic forces with much lead time.[2] Similarly, under current logging regimes, forest biomass and the critical carbon sequestration that our forests provide can be expected to increase substantially for at least the next one hundred years in most of the northeastern states. But it took shockingly little time to clear-cut the presettlement forests, and ten years ago I would not have forecast the current push by many groups to reestablish widespread clear-cutting to create young forest habitat for wildlife.

One of the obvious reasons for peering ahead is to avoid turbulent water. And there are many reasons to be alert. Our failure as a society to respond to the overwhelming evidence of the dire consequences of climate change suggests that humans are very good at avoiding taking predictions about the future seriously. If there is any lesson in the ecological history of northeastern forests, it is that a change in course can be inexorable and difficult to reverse once triggered. That climate change impacts on tree species may take centuries to play out doesn't mean they will be easy to reverse or even halt. The decimation of our tree species by pests and pathogens is, in principle, at least reversible, barring outright extinction of the tree species, but recovery would be measured in centuries if not millennia. Depletion of calcium from northeastern forest soils by acid rain could, in principle, be reversed at enormous expense by liming, but recovery of soil calcium from natural rates of soil weathering would, again, take centuries to millennia.

And unless there are major changes in international trade policies along the lines proposed by Tree-SMART Trade, it seems inevitable that more of our tree species will fall victim to new pests and pathogens. Red maple and sugar maple, the two most common tree species in eastern forests, make up roughly a quarter of all tree biomass outside of southern pine plantations. The maple genus (*Acer*) is large, with most of its species residing in the temperate forests of Asia. There is a correspondingly large community of insects and diseases that feed on or infect maples native to that region. It's hard not to walk in the woods without sensing that we have simply been lucky that the Asian longhorned beetles so destructive of red and sugar maple in the limited areas where they are currently being contained don't have the fecundity and dispersal ability of the emerald ash borers that are spreading like wildfire and decimating populations of ash trees. Who knows what traits the next imported forest pest or pathogen will have and which of our tree species they will attack? And the risk that climate change could make our native forest pests and pathogens more virulent and destructive remains very real.

So there is good reason for the doomsayer thread in much of the ecological research on the currents shaping northeastern forests. But there are also good reasons to respect the resilience of our tree species. They have been shaped over millions of years for tolerance of highly variable and often stressful environmental conditions, and we shouldn't underestimate their ability to either acclimate or take advantage of their genetic diversity and evolve to cope with new threats.

I am even more hopeful about the strength of the science being done to refine our understanding of the threats and find tools and the means to manage or at least cope with them. It's still a challenge to get scientists to work across the silos that are almost inevitable in addressing any complex ecological issue. And scaling up from the intricate detail coming out of modern genetic and molecular tools to understanding consequences at the level of populations and ecosystems is a very real challenge. But I see not only lots of interest within the scientific community in addressing those challenges but also an encouraging level of public interest in the effort. As risky as biological control can be, it is likely to become a valuable line of defense against forest pests and pathogens. There is inevitable tension between the pressures to quickly release potential control agents and the thorough science needed to ensure they don't wreak unintended havoc. That tug-of-war just makes it even more important to strengthen the science and be honest about the risks.

But the fact remains that there is enormous uncertainty when it comes to the future of our forests as well as very real limits on our ability to forecast change more than a few decades into the future. I see little support for the notion that our forests are resilient in the technical way that ecologists use that term, namely, that there are stabilizing mechanisms that steer the forests back to some predictable abundance of the component tree species. But it seems entirely appropriate to consider the tree species themselves as being resilient in the broader sense of the word. There is every reason to believe that the composition of our forests will continue to drift and even be buffeted in response to so many and such diverse forces. We should also expect that the pace of change will accelerate as the climate continues to warm. This has been touted as a hallmark of the new Anthropocene, but it is clear that the emergence of novel ecosystems has been in the works for centuries. It seems inescapable that our forests will be poorer in native species, at least until we figure out how to fight back against the spread of new pests and pathogens. And any change in the abundance of tree species has a cascading control over the rich array of ecosystem services that a forest provides.

I haven't entirely lost the admittedly naïve sense of wonder I had almost fifty years ago when I found that massive oak growing out of an old stone foundation. If anything, knowledge of the many currents at work makes me appreciate the seaworthiness of our forests even more.

Appendix: Common and Scientific Names of Northeastern Tree Species

The ornithologists and amateur birders have agreed on a standard set of common names matched to the formal scientific nomenclature for birds, but there is no such agreement for names of the trees of North America. I use common names of the trees in this book and have noted in parentheses where there is more than one common name in widespread usage. Scientific names consist of the genus, a specific epithet (the species within the genus), and the authority (crediting who first described the species with that particular name). Carl Linnaeus (1707–78) is the naming authority for more than a third of the species in the list below. Scientific names can change over time as taxonomists rework evolutionary lineages and either break previous species into finer categories or lump species into coarser groups that may show geographic variation but are still capable of fully interbreeding. Many of these tree species, however, occur across very large geographic regions and can be expected to show significant genetic variation across those ranges and in different environments. Some of the species within these genera are also capable of hybridizing.

Common name(s)	Scientific names
Balsam fir	*Abies balsamea* Mill.
Norway maple	*Acer pseudoplatanus* L.
Red maple	*Acer rubrum* L.
Sugar maple	*Acer saccharum* Marshall
Tree of heaven	*Ailanthus altissima* (Mill.) Swingle
Yellow birch	*Betula alleghaniensis* Britton
Black birch (Sweet birch)	*Betula lenta* L.
Paper birch (White birch)	*Betula papyrifera* Marshall
Musclewood	*Carpinus caroliniana* Walter
Bitternut hickory	*Carya cordiformis* (Wangenh.) K.Koch
Pignut hickory	*Carya glabra* Miller
Shagbark hickory	*Carya ovata* (Mill.) K.Koch
Mockernut hickory	*Carya tomentosa* (Lam.) Nutt.
Flowering dogwood	*Cornus florida* L.
American beech	*Fagus grandifolia* Ehrh.
White ash	*Fraxinus americana* L.
Black ash	*Fraxinus nigra* Marshall
Green ash	*Fraxinus pennsylvanica* Marshall
Butternut	*Juglans cinerea* L.
Black walnut	*Juglans nigra* L.
Eastern redcedar	*Juniperus virginiana* L.
Sweetgum	*Liquidambar styraciflua* L.
Tulip poplar (Yellow poplar)	*Liriodendron tulipifera* L.
Blackgum (Sour gum, Tupelo)	*Nyssa sylvatica* Marshall
Ironwood (Hophornbeam)	*Ostrya virginiana* (Mill.) K.Koch
Sourwood	*Oxydendrum arboreum* (L.) DC.
White spruce	*Picea glauca* (Moench) Voss
Red spruce	*Picea rubens* Sarg.
Jack pine	*Pinus banksiana* Lamb.
Red pine	*Pinus resinosa* Sol. ex Aiton

Eastern white pine	*Pinus strobus* L.
Balsam poplar	*Populus balsamifera* L.
Bigtooth aspen	*Populus grandidentata* Michx.
Quaking aspen (Trembling aspen)	*Populus tremuloides* Michx.
Black cherry	*Prunus serotina* Ehrh.
White oak	*Quercus alba* L.
Scarlet oak	*Quercus coccinea* Munchh.
Bur oak	*Quercus macrocarpa* Michx.
Chestnut oak	*Quercus montana* Willd.
Northern red oak	*Quercus rubra* L.
Black oak	*Quercus velutina* Lam.
Black locust	*Robinia pseudoacacia* L.
Sassafras	*Sassafras albidum* (Nutt.) Nees
Northern white cedar (Arborvitae)	*Thuja occidentalis* L.
American basswood	*Tilia americana* L.
Eastern hemlock	*Tsuga canadensis* (L.) Carrière
American elm	*Ulmus americana* L.
Slippery elm	*Ulmus rubra* Muhl.

Notes

1

Where Is the Crew, and Just What Ship Are We On, Anyway?

1. Federal agencies have been the driving force behind the U.S. National Vegetation Classification and Standard (http://usnvc.org/overview). This makes sense because they manage a broad range of ecosystems and have an understandable need to summarize and communicate information about them. On the other hand, I have never encountered ecological research published in peer-review scientific literature that used the system. Forest ecologists appear to be stubbornly resistant to standardizing their naming conventions.

2. Henry A. Gleason's ideas about the individualistic distribution of species were published in Henry A. Gleason, "The Individualistic Concept of the Plant Association," *Bulletin of the Torrey Botanical Club* 53, no. 1 (1926): 7–26. The work of John T. Curtis and his early students was summarized in the classic and still valuable 1959 book *The Vegetation of Wisconsin—An Ordination of Plant Communities* (Madison: University of Wisconsin Press). Robert H. Whittaker's classic work was on the distribution of species along elevation gradients in the Santa Catalina Mountains of Arizona, the Siskiyou Mountains of Oregon, and the Great Smoky Mountains of the southern Appalachians.

3. Ecologists use a wide variety of often extraordinarily arcane multivariate statistical methods to characterize variability in the species composition found in a sample of plots. The use of these "ordination" methods grew out of the work of John Curtis at Wisconsin and particularly under the guidance of Robert Whittaker while he was at Cornell. The distance between points, that is, sample plots, in the ordination is a measure of their similarity

in species composition. Most vegetation studies involve going out and choosing plots to sample on the basis of preconceptions of the community types the investigator is interested in. In such studies the points in the ordination typically cluster into the chosen vegetation types. But if you sample randomly across the landscape and thereby fully represent the true variability in forest composition, an ordination will typically show a much more uniform cloud of points, with very little clustering into discrete community types. For an example see Charles D. Canham, Michael J. Papaik, Maria Uriarte, William H. McWilliams, Jennifer C. Jenkins, and Mark J. Twery, "Neighborhood Analyses of Canopy Tree Competition along Environmental Gradients in New England Forests," *Ecological Applications* 16, no. 2 (2006): 540–54.

4. The maps in figures 1 and 2 ignore the abundance of many of those species in the eastern Canadian provinces. For example, some of the species of oaks and hickories sneak up through the Champlain Valley and spill over into the low elevations of the St. Lawrence Valley of Quebec.

5. Given the high, prolonged duration of deposition of nitrogen from air pollution, ecologists in the Northeast have become increasingly interested in whether there are signs that phosphorus is becoming more important as a limiting nutrient. For a compendium of data on foliar chemistry in northeastern forests and what it can tell us about nutrient limitation, see K. F. Crowley, B. E. McNeil, G. M. Lovett, C. D. Canham, C. T. Driscoll, L. E. Rustad, E. Denny, R. A. Hallett, M. A. Arthur, J. L. Boggs, C. L. Goodale, J. S. Kahl, S. G. McNulty, S. V. Ollinger, L. H. Pardo, P. G. Schaberg, J. L. Stoddard, M. P. Weand, and K. C. Weathers, "Do Nutrient Limitation Patterns Shift from Nitrogen Toward Phosphorus with Increasing Nitrogen Deposition Across the Northeastern United States?" *Ecosystems* 15 (2012): 940–57. The upshot from that study is that there is some reason for interest in phosphorus but that nitrogen remains more important in most forests.

A number of approaches have been used to estimate the fraction of the nitrogen that falls on a forest that is retained within the forest rather than being exported downslope into streams, lakes, and rivers. My own work with colleagues on nutrient loading to Adirondack lakes led to an estimate that, on average, 87 percent of nitrogen deposition on upland forests was being retained rather than transported to lakes in each watershed. This is an incredibly important benefit for those lakes. See Charles D. Canham, Michael. L. Pace, Kathleen C. Weathers, Edward W. McNeil, Barbara L. Bedford, Lora Murphy, and Scott Quinn, "Nitrogen Deposition and Lake Nitrogen Concentrations: A Regional Analysis of Terrestrial Controls and Aquatic Linkages," *Ecosphere* 3, no. 7 (2012): 66, http://dx.doi.org/10.1890/ES12-00090.1

John Aber and colleagues, in a 1989 paper, focused attention on the potential for nitrogen saturation due to excess inputs traced to nitrous oxide emissions from power plants. Both the northeastern United States and most of western Europe were receiving high inputs because of the concentration of power plants upwind. Their paper outlined a fairly dire set of predicted consequences. Almost thirty years later there is still cause for concern, but research has uncovered previously unknown ways in which forest soils can absorb that nitrogen (hopefully without ill effects). See John D. Aber, Knute J. Nadelhoffer, Paul Steudler, and Jerry M. Melillo, "Nitrogen Saturation in Northern Forest Ecosystems," *Bioscience* 39 (1989): 378–86, https://doi .org/10.2307/1311067.

6. See Canham et al., "Neighborhood Analyses of Canopy Tree Competition," and Michael J. Papaik and Charles D. Canham, "Multi-Model Analysis of Tree Competition along Environmental Gradients in Southern New England Forests," *Ecological Applications* 16, no. 5 (2006): 1880–92.

2
Charting a Course

1. Eugene P. Odum, "The Strategy of Ecosystem Development," *Science* 164 (1969): 262–70.

2. Henry C. Cowles (1869–1939) did the classic work on primary succession on Lake Michigan sand dunes for his doctoral thesis in 1898. One of his students, William S. Cooper (1884–1978), began work on primary succession at Glacier Bay in Alaska in 1916. The Glacier Bay studies have been maintained by a succession of later ecologists. Frank Egler's wager is reprinted in a letter written by him dated July 20, 1981 in *Bulletin of the Ecological Society of America* 62, no. 4 (1981): 230–31. He made the wager almost impossible to meet by requiring "at least five stages, as indicated in diagrams published by me, in the sequence referred to as classical Relay Floristics." Egler's alternative to relay floristics was known as "initial floristics." Egler was one of W. S. Cooper's many graduate students.

3. Henry Horn's monograph on the adaptive geometry of trees had an enormous influence on my thinking about tree architecture. He used simple, crude methods to visually estimate differences in the shade cast by trees of different shade tolerance and crown architecture. More than twenty years after his work, colleagues and I used a lot of expensive equipment and time in the forest to quantify the patterns he observed. See Henry S. Horn, *The Adaptive Geometry of Trees* (Princeton: Princeton University Press, 1971);

and Charles D. Canham, Adrien C. Finzi, Stephen W. Pacala, and Diane H. Burbank, "Causes and Consequences of Resource Heterogeneity in Forests—Interspecific Variation in Light Transmission by Canopy Trees," *Canadian Journal of Forest Research–Revue canadienne de recherche forestière* 24, no. 2 (1994): 337–49.

4. The classic reference on shade tolerance rankings is Frederick S. Baker, "A Revised Tolerance Table," *Journal of Forestry* 47 (1949): 179–81. A more recent table based on Baker's original ranking is provided in Ülo Niinemets and Fernando Valladares, "Tolerance to Shade, Drought, and Waterlogging of Temperate Northern Hemisphere Trees and Shrubs," *Ecological Monographs* 76 (2006): 521–47. The method Richard Kobe and Stephen Pacala devised to measure shade tolerance is described in Richard K. Kobe, Stephen W. Pacala, John A. Silander, and Charles D. Canham, "Juvenile Tree Survivorship as a Component of Shade Tolerance," *Ecological Applications* 5 (1995): 517–32.

5. David Tilman of the University of Minnesota presented theoretical models and field data from grasslands and herbaceous communities related to the notion that the competitive dominant in a system was the species that could tolerate depleting a critical resource to a level lower than all other competitors. His emphasis was on soil resources, and the hypothesis with respect to soil resources has had only ambivalent support. See David Tilman, *Resource Competition and Community Structure* (Princeton: Princeton University Press, 1982).

6. Sugar maple and beech saplings have different architectural tricks to help minimize, as they get bigger, the metabolic costs of building and maintaining the branches they need to display leaves tailored to either the very low light beneath a closed canopy or the higher light levels found in gaps. See Charles D. Canham, "Growth and Canopy Architecture of Shade-Tolerant Trees—Response to Canopy Gaps," *Ecology* 69 (1988): 786–95. Nonetheless, the rising metabolic costs that a sapling faces as it gets bigger in deep shade appear inexorable. Daniel Kneeshaw and Richard Kobe extended Kobe's original method of estimating sapling survival as a function of growth to include explicit consideration of sapling size. For five of the six species they examined, shade tolerance, as quantified by survival at low growth rates, declined with increasing size of the sapling. See Daniel D. Kneeshaw, Richard K. Kobe, K. David Coates, and Christian Messier, "Sapling Size Influences Shade Tolerance Ranking Among Southern Boreal Tree Species," *Journal of Ecology* 94 (2006): 471–80.

7. Richard K. Kobe, "Intraspecific Variation in Sapling Mortality and Growth Predicts Geographic Variation in Forest Composition," *Ecological Monographs* 66 (1996): 181–201.

8. The notion of the importance of forest gaps dates at least as far back as A. S. Watt's early (1925) work on beech forests in England, summarized in his 1947 article "Pattern and Process in the Plant Community," *Journal of Ecology* 35 (1947): 1–22. Simon Levin presented the most widely cited formal mathematical model for gap dynamics in a paper in 1974 coauthored with Robert Paine titled "Disturbance, Patch Formation, and Community Structure," *Proceedings of the National Academy of Sciences* 71 (1974): 2744–47. While written with reference to patch dynamics in rocky intertidal communities, their ideas translated easily to the dynamics of gaps in forest canopies.

9. The opening of even a small gap in the canopy has immediate effects not just on understory light but also on soil nutrients. The effects on those different resources, however, are not spatially congruent. The highest light levels are under the canopy to the north of the edge of the gap. But that is also one of the driest spots for seedlings because of higher light and associated temperatures and because of the presence of the root system of the tree overhead. The highest soil nitrogen availability occurs in the center of the gap due to reduced uptake there as a result of the death of the tree that died to create the gap.

There is a simple relationship between latitude and the maximum elevation angle of the sun above the southern horizon (i.e., at solar noon): elevation = 90 – latitude (in degrees) + declination. Declination varies daily from –23.45 on the winter solstice to 23.45 on the summer solstice. Thus for a given latitude the maximum elevation, or angle above the horizon, reached by the sun at any point in the year is equal to 113.45 – latitude. Thus at 45° N latitude the sun is never higher than 68.45° above the horizon, and a point in the understory needs to be roughly ten meters north of the south edge of a gap in a twenty-five-meter-tall canopy to receive any direct sunlight through the gap. Single tree gaps in old-growth northern forests are rarely much more than ten meters in diameter.

10. See Charles D. Canham, "Suppression and Release during Canopy Recruitment in *Acer saccharum*," *Bulletin of the Torrey Botanical Club* 112 (1985): 134–45; and Charles D. Canham, "Suppression and Release during Canopy Recruitment in *Fagus grandifolia*," *Bulletin of the Torrey Botanical Club* 117 (1990): 1–7. Someone once told me he couldn't believe I got these papers published, based as they were on such a small sample size (ten trees of each of the two species in each of three stands) and using none of the elaborate, arcane statistical methods normally used for analysis of tree rings. But they are two of my favorites among the papers I've written. They tied together a number of threads of research into a story that to my mind has stood the test of time.

11. The most comprehensive reference for the natural history and ecology of North American tree species is Russell M. Burns and Barbara H. Honkala, *Silvics of North America: 1. Conifers; 2. Hardwoods* (Agriculture Handbook 654, US Department of Agriculture, Forest Service, Washington, DC). It contains detailed descriptions of the native ranges, climate, soils, associated forest cover types, and life histories of over two hundred species. It is more than a bit dated, but I have a well-worn and still-used copy in my office. The manual is now more commonly accessed online: https://www.srs .fs.usda.gov/pubs/misc/ag_654/table_of_contents.htm.

12. Richard Kobe and Eric Ribbens in 1995, Jim Hill, Adrien Finzi, and Jim Hill in 1996, and John Casperson in 1998 were the first cohort of graduate students to work at Great Mountain Forest on the development of the SORTIE model. All received their doctoral degrees from the University of Connecticut. Later graduate students who worked on this research included Jaclyn Schnurr (PhD, Idaho State University), Christopher Tripler (PhD, Idaho State University), Michael Papaik (PhD, University of Massachusetts), Feike Dijkstra (PhD, University of Wageningen), and Natasja van Gestel (MS, University of Wageningen).

13. One direct method to estimate the effective dispersal distance a seed can travel away from a tree is to search for a single individual of a species in a stand at a location with no others of that species anywhere nearby. Then you can put out baskets along transects away from the tree in different directions and count the numbers of seeds (or seedlings, for that matter) found at given distances away. A plot of the numbers of seeds found as a function of distance from a tree is known as a seed shadow. This method is rarely practical, however, not least because of the difficulty of finding isolated individuals of more common species. Eric Ribbens and Stephen Pacala inverted the problem and proposed a method that involves placing seed baskets or quadrats to count seedlings throughout a stand. They then mapped the spatial distributions of all of the trees in the stand and used statistical methods to solve for the shapes of the seed or seedling shadows that would best explain (or maximize the likelihood, in technical terms) the observed distributions of seeds or seedlings, given the overlapping seed shadows of the different adult trees of a given species. The method has since been applied to the study of seed and seedling distributions in forests worldwide. See Eric Ribbens, John A. Silander, and Stephen W. Pacala, "Seedling Recruitment in Forests— Calibrating Models to Predict Patterns of Tree Seedling Dispersion," *Ecology* 75, no. 6 (1994): 1794–1806.

14. Stephen W. Pacala, Charles D. Canham, John Saponara, John A. Silander Jr., Richard K. Kobe, and Eric Ribbens, "Forest Models Defined by

Field Measurements: Estimation, Error Analysis and Dynamics," *Ecological Monographs* 66, no. 1 (1996): 1–43.

15. David Coates (British Columbia Forest Service, retired) and Christian Messier (University of Quebec) have coauthored with Klaus Puettmann (Oregon State University) *A Critique of Silviculture: Managing for Complexity* (Washington, DC: Island Press, 2008). The book critiques the traditional agricultural model of forestry with its emphasis on even-aged management of monocultures and argues for greater incorporation of ecology and recognition of the value of complexity in the practice of silviculture.

16. The structure of the original model, named SORTIE, was hardwired into the computer code. That approach quickly became too cumbersome to adapt to new questions and forests, so Lora Murphy, Michael Papaik, and I jettisoned the original code and devised a new architecture that would allow essentially unlimited extension of the spatially explicit, individual-tree-based approach. The new model, called SORTIE-ND (for Neighborhood Dynamics) (www.sortie-nd.org), is basically a framework that any researcher can modify by adding new behaviors. Murphy has been responsible for almost all of the code development, documentation, and management of the website, where the model is freely available to any who want to use it.

17. Because of their mobility and response to larger-scale habitat conditions, animals can easily create exceptions to the typically small effective neighborhoods that influence the fate of a tree. For example, winter deer yards in a dense hemlock stand result in very heavy browse pressure on seedlings and saplings. But a good winter deer yard is generally much larger than twenty meters across.

18. See Adrien C. Finzi and Charles D. Canham, "Non-Additive Effects of Litter Mixtures on Net N Mineralization in a Southern New England Forest," *Forest Ecology and Management* 105, no. 1–3 (1998): 129–36; and Seth Bigelow and Charles Canham, "Neighborhood-Scale Analyses of Non-Additive Species Effects on Cation Concentrations in Forest Soils," *Ecosystems* 20 (2017): 1351–63.

3
Home Port

1. Lake sediments are typically dated by means of radiocarbon methods that measure the concentration of the ^{14}C isotope in organic material in the sediment. But converting from a date calculated by this method to an actual calendar year requires a calibration procedure, and those procedures are the

subject of continual improvement, so I have simply used the originally reported radiocarbon dates given in figures 6 and 7.

2. Pollen preserved in lake sediments can often be identified only to the
level of genus or subgenus, not individual species. But for many important
species, including beech, hemlock, and chestnut, only one member of the
genus is present in the region, so there is no ambiguity. The basic patterns of
earliest arrival and subsequent changes in abundance of these taxa are known
from dozens of studies at different lakes throughout the northeastern United
States. Margaret Davis was the first prominent proponent of the notion that
innate limitations in dispersal and migration rates might have been responsible for some of the pattern. More recent studies tend to emphasize climatic controls alone, for example, Bryan Shuman, Paige Newby, Yongsung
Huang, and Thompson Webb III, "Evidence for Close Climatic Control of
New England Vegetation History," *Ecology* 85 (2004): 1297–1310. For a
number of reasons palynologists favor climatic explanations, but to my mind
there are still viable alternative or additional explanations and very real
limitations on the certainty with which we can explain any of the patterns.

3. Donald R. Whitehead and Stephen T. Jackson, "The Regional Vegetational History of the High Peaks (Adirondack Mountains) New York," *New
York State Museum Bulletin,* no. 478 (1990): ISBN 1–55557–195–6. See also
Stephen T. Jackson and Donald R. Whitehead, "Holocene Vegetation Patterns
in the Adirondack Mountains," *Ecology* 72 (1991): 641–53.

4. Terryanne E. Maenza-Gmelch, "Late-Glacial—Early Holocene Vegetation, Climate, and Fire at Sutherland Pond, Hudson Highlands, Southeastern New York, U.S.A." *Canadian Journal of Botany* 75 (1997): 431–39.

5. Paleoecologists have always informed their interpretations of histori-
cal patterns with an understanding of contemporary ecological processes.
Stephen Jackson's research and writing take this further than most. For a
recent example, see Stephen T. Jackson and Jessica L. Blois, "Community
Ecology in a Changing Environment: Perspectives from the Quaternary,"
*Proceedings of the National Academy of Sciences of the United States of
America* 112 (2015): 4915–21.

6. See David R. Foster, W. Wyatt Oswald, Edward K. Faison, Elaine D.
Doughty, and Barbara C. S. Hansen, "A Climatic Driver for Abrupt Mid-
Holocene Vegetation Dynamics and the Hemlock Decline in New England,"
Ecology 87 (2006): 2959–66. Recent research has refined our understanding
of the exact timing and spatial pattern of the hemlock decline. It's clear that
hemlocks did not completely disappear from the landscape and presumably
survived at low abundance or in isolated pockets. A paper by Lindsay Day
and colleagues looks at the sizes of the hemlock pollen grains in the sediments

as an indication of distance to the source trees, on the assumption that smaller grains came from farther away. See Lindsay T. Day, W. Wyatt Oswald, Elaine D. Doughty, and David. R. Foster, "Analysis of Hemlock Pollen Size in Holocene Lake Sediments from New England," *Quaternary Research* 79 (2013): 362–65.

7. Jennifer C. Jenkins, Charles D. Canham, and Paul K. Barton, "Predicting Long-Term Forest Development Following Hemlock Mortality," in Katherine A. McManus, Kathleen S. Shields, and Dennis R. Souto, eds., "Proceedings: Symposium on Sustainable Management of Hemlock Ecosystems in Eastern North America," *USDA Forest Service General Technical Report NE-267*, 62–75 (Newtown Square, PA: US Department of Agriculture, 2000).

8. The end of the Pleistocene saw the extinction of ninety genera of mammals in North America, including all species larger than our current-day bison. I frankly find it hard to believe that either climate change or the arrival of human hunters alone could have wrought such a calamitous change. But it is even more surprising to me that we have little evidence that the extinction of this vast assemblage of animals, including species like mastodons, which are assumed to have been forest dwellers, had significant impact on the nature of the early postglacial forests. For an example of how ecologists have studied this issue, see Guy S. Robinson, Lida Pigott Burney, and David A. Burney, "Landscape Paleoecology and Megafaunal Extinction in Southeastern New York State," *Ecological Monographs* 75 (2005): 295–315. For an example of how ecologists have explored the potential longer-term impacts of Native Americans on forest composition, see Stephen J. Tulowiecki and Chris P. S. Larsen, "Native American Impact on Past Forest Composition Inferred from Species Distribution Models, Chautauqua County, New York," *Ecological Monographs* 85 (2015): 557–81.

9. Using survey records for portions of Maine, Craig Lorimer published the first estimate of rates of disturbance of presettlement forests by wind. Orie Loucks and I then did a similar analysis for the state of Wisconsin. Lisa Schulte and David Mladenoff revisited the Wisconsin records with a more detailed analysis. But all of these are limited to analysis of only the most catastrophic disturbance in which most of the canopy was toppled. See Craig G. Lorimer, "The Presettlement Forest and Natural Disturbance Cycle of Northeastern Maine," *Ecology* 58 (1977): 139–48; Charles D. Canham and Orie L. Loucks, "Catastrophic Windthrow in the Presettlement Forests of Wisconsin," *Ecology* 65 (1984): 803–9; and Lisa A. Schulte and David J. Mladenoff, "Severe Wind and Fire Regimes in Northern Forests: Historical Variability at the Regional Scale," *Ecology* 86 (2005): 431–45.

10. Witness tree records have been used by ecologists for almost a century. Charles Cogbill has been the driving force behind assembling these records for the Northeast and particularly New England, focusing on the early town proprietor surveys. Peter Marks and colleagues have reconstructed patterns from surveys of the Military Tract in central New York, created after the Revolutionary War to repay soldiers and encourage settlement. Ecologists in the upper Midwest have the luxury of working with the more detailed and systematic (and better archived) nineteenth-century surveys of the US General Land Office. For examples, see Charles V. Cogbill, John Burk, and G. Motzkin, "The Forests of Presettlement New England, USA: Spatial and Compositional Patterns Based on Town Proprietor Surveys," *Journal of Biogeography* 29 (2002): 1279–1304; and Peter L. Marks and Sana Gardescu, "Vegetation of the Central Finger Lakes Region of New York in the 1790s," *New York State Museum Bulletin,* no. 484 (1992): ISBN 1–55557–225–1.

The standardized nineteenth-century land survey methods used under the US General Land Office to open up new territories for settlement in the Midwest make it possible to calculate reasonably quantitative estimates of species abundance and forest structure at the time of the surveys. This invites quantitative comparison with modern forests via sources such as the current forest inventory plots maintained by the US Forest Service. Examples of this work include Simon J. Goring, David J. Mladenoff, Charles V. Cogbill, Sydne Record, Christopher J. Paciorek, Stephen T. Jackson, Michael C. Dietze, Andria Dawson, Jaclyn Hatala Matthes, Jason S. McLachlan, and John W. Williams, "Novel and Lost Forests in the Upper Midwestern United States, from New Estimates of Settlement-Era Composition, Stem Density, and Biomass," *PLoS ONE* 11, no. 12 (2016): e0151935. doi:10.1371/journal. pone.0151935. The earlier survey methods in New England provide less precise information on forest structure but still allow estimation of change. See Jonathan R. Thompson, Dunbar N. Carpenter, Charles V. Cogbill, and David R. Foster, "Four Centuries of Change in Northeastern United States Forests," *PLoS ONE* 8, no. 9 (2013): e72540. doi:10.1371/journal.pone.0072540.

11. See Goring et al. cited in "Novel and Lost Forests."

4

Legacies of Agricultural Clearing and Early Logging

1. https://www.monticello.org/site/house-and-gardens/hessian-fly.

2. Peter L. Marks, "On the Origin of the Field Plants of the Northeastern United States," *American Naturalist* 122 (1983): 210–28.

3. For example, a study by Rhine Singleton and colleagues found that forests on land that had been abandoned from agriculture sixty to ninety years earlier still had an herbaceous layer that was lower in abundance, richness, and diversity than in nearby stands that had never been cleared for agriculture. Rhine Singleton, Sana Gardescu, Peter L. Marks, and Monica A. Geber, "Forest Herb Colonization of Postagricultural Forests in Central New York State, USA," *Journal of Ecology* 89 (2001): 325–38.

4. The writings of the American botanist John Bartram (1699–1777) and the Swedish botanist Peter (Pehr) Kalm (1716–79) are standard references for the early natural history of the American colonies. Bartram traveled extensively, from Florida to Lake Ontario and west to the Ohio River. Kalm spent the years from 1748 to 1751 traveling the northeastern colonies. While early colonists were busily introducing many new plant species to the Americas, Bartram was just as busy sending seeds of our native plants to England.

5. The history of the early tanning industry in New York is a classic story of boom and bust. Hemlock bark was the best early source of the tannins needed in the process, and because animal hides could be more easily transported than hemlock bark tanneries sprang up all across the Catskills in the early 1800s, while the hides were imported from as far away as South America. But by the 1840s hemlocks had been stripped from the slopes of the Catskills, and the tanneries moved north to hemlock forests in the foothills of the Adirondacks. That supply was rapidly exhausted as well. Barbara Mc-Martin's wonderful book *Hides, Hemlocks and Adirondack History* (Utica: North Country Books, 1992) notes that there were over 150 tanneries in the Adirondacks in 1850 but that the industry had largely disappeared by 1890.

6. Robert McIntosh published one of the early reconstructions of changes in forest composition using witness tree data from original land surveys. His analysis of changes in forests of the Catskills noted that the hemlocks that had been abundant at the time of settlement had not recovered from the heavy logging they experienced during the tanning industry boom there in the early 1800s. Robert P. McIntosh, "The Forest Cover of the Catskill Mountain Region, New York, as Indicated by Land Survey Records," *American Midland Naturalist* 68 (1962): 409–23.

5
Seared into Memory

1. Timothy Egan, *The Big Burn* (Boston: Houghton Mifflin Harcourt, 2009)

2. Miron L. Heinselman, "Fire in the Virgin Forests of the Boundary Waters Canoe Area, Minnesota," *Quaternary Research* 3 (1973): 329–82. Soon after publishing his pioneering research on fire regimes of the upper Midwest, Heinselman retired from the Forest Service to devote his time to securing federal wilderness protection for the Boundary Waters. This was accomplished in 1978 with the designation of the Boundary Waters Canoe Area.

3. While crown fires were infrequent in typical upland forests, particularly in the northern forests, some of the most diverse and biologically unique forests in the region are the fire-dependent pine barrens that occur either on deep sands or on very thin soils over a rock "pavement." The most extensive of these are the pitch pine barrens of southern New Jersey, eastern Long Island, Cape Cod, and near Albany. Conservation organizations and state agencies have done extraordinarily important work to preserve these ecosystems and maintain the fire regimes without which these ecosystems would disappear, replaced by more fire-sensitive species. The truly unique pitch pine pavement barrens along the Shawangunk Ridge of New York (see fig. 10) and scattered jack pine barrens much farther north have been a much greater challenge since they are often found in smaller patches and the politics of maintaining the necessary fire regime are much more problematic.

4. Gordon Day prepared a detailed compendium of early reports of land clearing and use of fire by Native Americans, written from the perspective of an ecologist nearly seventy years ago. I have no idea how modern anthropologists would interpret the same material. See Gordon M. Day, "The Indian as an Ecological Factor in the Northeastern Forest," *Ecology* 34 (1953): 329–46. Emily Russell Southgate's review disputes the conclusion that fires were widespread, arguing that they were restricted to the periphery of settlements. Emily W. B. Russell, "Indian-Set Fires in the Forests of Northeastern United States," *Ecology* 64 (1983): 78–88. She explores the broader challenge of incorporating historical research in ecology in her book *People and the Land through Time: Linking Ecology and History*, 2nd ed. (New Haven: Yale University Press, 2019).

5. Marc Abrams's work has highlighted the extraordinary adaptability of red maple. His 1998 paper reviews the factors that could explain the dramatic expansion in the distribution and abundance of red maple following European settlement. See Marc D. Abrams, "The Red Maple Paradox," *Bioscience* 48 (1998): 355–63.

6. Patrick H. Brose, Daniel C. Dey, and Thomas A. Waldrop, "The Fire-Oak Literature of Eastern North America: Synthesis and Guidelines," *USDA Forest Service General Technical Report NRS-135* (2014). This synthesis focuses on providing guidelines for the use of prescribed fire to restore upland oak forests.·

7. Ryan W. McEwan, James M. Dyer, and Neil Pederson, "Multiple Interacting Ecosystem Drivers: Toward an Encompassing Hypothesis of Oak Forest Dynamics across Eastern North America," *Ecography* 34 (2011): 244–56. This paper challenges the primary focus on the role of fire in oak forests, arguing that more attention should be focused on the role of drought. But arguing that ecologists were too preoccupied with fire in oak forests was a bit of a straw man in 2011. Despite its title, Marc Abrams's widely cited 1992 paper on fire and oak forests takes a very broad view of the factors that have influenced the distribution and dynamics of oak forests. See Marc D. Abrams, "Fire and the Development of Oak Forests," *Bioscience* 42 (1992): 346–53.

6
The Fall and Rise of the White-Tailed Deer

1. Elk have a powerful lobby in elk hunters and have been reintroduced in several parts of the East. A recent report focuses on the challenges of restraining the exceptional success of the introductions, with estimates of a current population of over ten thousand elk in southeastern Kentucky. I know of no attempts to reintroduce woodland bison in the East, but hope springs eternal. See John J. Cox, "Tales of a Repatriated Megaherbivore: Challenges and Opportunities in the Management of Reintroduced Elk in Appalachia," in Songlin Fei, John M. Lhotka, Jeffrey W. Stringer, Kurt W. Gottschalk, and Gary W. Miller, eds., *Proceedings, 17th Central Hardwood Forest Conference; 2010 April 5–7; Lexington, KY*, General Technical Report NRS-P-78, 632–42 (Newtown Square, PA: US Department of Agriculture, Forest Service, Northern Research Station, 2011).

2. In 1909 Ernest Thompson Seton published the first widely cited estimate of pre-European white-tailed deer density in the eastern United States (~4 deer/square kilometer). McCabe and McCabe revisited the subject in 1984 and came up with very close to the same number. See R. E. McCabe and T. R. McCabe, "Of Slings and Arrows: An Historical Retrospection," in Lowell K. Halls, ed., *White-Tailed Deer Ecology and Management*, 19–72 (Harrisburg, PA: Stackpole, 1984). The estimate of the density of white-tailed deer in the Catskill Mountains of New York in the late 1880s is cited in C. W. Severinghouse and C. P. Brown, "History of the White-Tailed Deer in New York," *New York Fish and Game Journal* 3 (1956): 129–67.

3. It is hard to find reliable estimates of actual deer densities across significant portions of the animal's range. Wildlife agencies use a variety of relative indices of abundance to set management guidelines, but it is often difficult to

translate these into a true density estimate or, because of differences in methods, to apply them across state boundaries. The estimates used in the peer-reviewed scientific literature tend to come from a small number of studies in relatively small study areas. A commonly used estimate of the number of pellet groups an adult deer produces per day over the winter comes from David S. deCalesta, "Reliability and Precision of Pellet-Group Counts for Estimating Landscape-Level Deer Density," *Human–Wildlife Interactions* 7 (2013): 60–68.

4. There is a large literature documenting rates of browsing on saplings of different species of trees. The results are usually couched in terms of assessing deer preferences and food choice. But results vary widely among the studies, presumably because different forests present widely diverse food choices. Examples of such studies include Lauren Bradshaw and Donald M. Waller, "Impacts of White-Tailed Deer on Regional Patterns of Forest Tree Recruitment," *Forest Ecology and Management* 375 (2016): 1–11. See also François Potvin, Pierre Beaupré, and Gaétan Laprise, "The Eradication of Balsam Fir Stands by White-Tailed Deer on Anticosti Island, Québec: A 150-Year Process," *Ecoscience* 10 (2003): 487–95. I compiled data from US Forest Service Forest Inventory and Analysis plots for the states of Vermont and New Hampshire to calculate the relative abundance of balsam fir and red spruce in both the sapling layer and in the canopy in those two states.

5. The early work reporting effects of forest fertilization on deer browsing can be found in H. L. Mitchell and N. W. Hosley, "Differential Browsing by Deer on Plots Variously Fertilized," *Black Rock Forest Bulletin* 1, no. 5 (1936). A much later study exploring the same issue is reported in C. E. Tripler, C. D. Canham, R. S. Inouye, and J. L. Schnurr, "Soil Nitrogen Availability, Plant Luxury Consumption, and Herbivory by White-Tailed Deer," *Oecologia* 133 (2002): 517–24.

6. For a sample of studies, see David S. deCalesta, "Effect of White-Tailed Deer on Songbirds Within Managed Forests in Pennsylvania," *Journal of Wildlife Management* 58 (1994): 711–18; Thomas P. Rooney, "High White-Tailed Deer Densities Benefit Graminoids and Contribute to Biotic Homogenization of Forest Ground-Layer Vegetation," *Plant Ecology* 202 (2009): 103–11; and Tiffany M. Knight, Jessica L. Dunn, Lisa A. Smith, JoAnn Davis, and Susan Kalisz, "Deer Facilitate Invasive Plant Success in a Pennsylvania Forest Understory," *Natural Areas Journal* 29 (2009): 110–16.

7. The evidence for a link between hayscented fern abundance and high deer densities comes from exclosure studies that have shown lower fern abundance inside exclosures. The actual mechanism behind the link is not directly addressed by exclosure studies but presumably reflects both direct effects of low palatability of the ferns and release of the ferns from competi-

tion with other understory herbs and shrubs that are preferentially browsed by deer. But dense layers of hayscented fern generally require a canopy opening or disturbance to first get established. Once established, they can persist for a long time, even after deer densities decline. See James D. Hill and John A. Silander Jr., "Distribution and Dynamics of Two Ferns: *Dennstaedtia punctilobula* (Dennstaedtiaceae) and *Thelypteris noveboracensis* (Thelypteridaceae) in a Northeast Mixed Hardwoods–Hemlock Forest," *American Journal of Botany* 88 (2001): 894–902; and Tim Nuttle, Todd E. Ristau, and Alejandro A. Royo, "Long-Term Biological Legacies of Herbivore Density in a Landscape-Scale Experiment: Forest Understoreys Reflect Past Deer Density Treatments for at Least 20 Years," *Journal of Ecology* 102 (2014): 221–28. There has been a lot of research on the effects of fern layers on tree regenerations. Two examples are Lisa O. George and F. A. Bazzaz, "The Fern Understory as an Ecological Filter: Growth and Survival of Canopy-Tree Seedlings," *Ecology* 80 (1999): 846–56; and Lisa O. George and F. A. Bazzaz, "The Fern Understory as an Ecological Filter: Emergence and Establishment of Canopy-Tree Seedlings," *Ecology* 80 (1999): 833–45.

8. Duane R. Diefenbach, William L. Palmer, and William K. Shope, "Attitudes of Pennsylvania Sportsmen Towards Managing White-Tailed Deer to Protect the Ecological Integrity of Forests," *Wildlife Society Bulletin* 25 (1997): 244–51.

9. The first controlled hunt on the Cary Institute property took place in 1970. Over time the goals and methods of the program have evolved. By 1976 hunters had to possess a state-issued antlerless deer permit to participate. Effects of the program have been documented through extensive data on hunter participation and effort, the annual deer harvest, and annual surveys of deer browse in Cary Institute forests. For a general description of the program, see Raymond J. Winchcombe, "Controlled Access Hunting for Deer Population Management: A Case Study," *Northeast Wildlife* 50 (1993): 1–9.

10. A study by Howard Kilpatrick and colleagues documents changes in home range size and configuration as a result of an intensive effort to reduce astronomically high deer densities in an eight-hundred-acre park in Connecticut. Their results led them to conclude that localized controlled hunts could be effective in an area of that size. The Cary Institute controlled hunt occurs on a property close to two thousand acres in size. See Howard J. Kilpatrick, Shelley M. Spohr, and Kelly K. Lima, "Effects of Population Reduction on Home Ranges of Female White-Tailed Deer at High Densities," *Canadian Journal of Zoology* 79 (2001): 949–54.

11. A number of websites are devoted to the Young Forest Initiative. For example, see https://youngforest.org.

12. A 2017 study tried to quantify the benefits of reintroduction of cougars in the eastern United States as a means to reduce white-tailed deer density, not in terms of the benefits to forest health but in terms of the reduction in human injuries, fatalities, and property damage due to reductions in deer–vehicle collisions. It is framed as a "first valuation of an ecosystem service provided by large carnivore recolonization." But the take-home message was much more direct: the authors estimated that the reestablishment of cougars in the eastern United States would reduce deer densities by roughly 20 percent with a corresponding reduction in deer–vehicle collisions, preventing more than 21,000 human injuries, more than 150 fatalities, and more than $2 billion in avoided costs within thirty years. The reduction in human fatalities was a net benefit after acknowledgment that there is an extraordinarily low but nonzero rate of human fatality from cougar attacks. See Sophie L. Gilbert, Kelly J. Sivy, Casey B. Pozzanghera, Adam DuBour, Kelly Overduijn, Matthew M. Smith, Jiake Zhou, Joseph M. Little, and Laura R. Prugh, "Socioeconomic Benefits of Large Carnivore Recolonization Through Reduced Wildlife–Vehicle Collisions," *Conservation Letters* 10 (2017): 431–39.

7

A Sea Change in Logging

1. The vast majority of ecological research on logging has focused on detrimental environmental impacts. In contrast, I think it is fair to say that both academic and practicing foresters are motivated by a conviction that their actions improve forest health. I've long felt that these very different perspectives reflect diametrically opposed but very deep-seated beliefs about the proper role of humans in nature.

2. I was not alone as an ecologist in originally focusing on unmanaged forests; the ecological literature is full of studies that summarize causes of tree mortality in eastern forests but completely omit consideration of losses to logging. Recent examples include a number of major studies designed to assess the potential responses of eastern forests to climate change. See Mark C. Vanderwel, David A. Coomes, and Drew W. Purves, "Quantifying Variation in Forest Disturbance, and Its Effects on Aboveground Biomass Dynamics, Across the Eastern United States," *Global Change Biology* 19 (2013): 1504–17. My colleagues' and my estimate of the fraction of regional adult tree mortality due to harvesting would have obviously been much higher if we had included the southeastern forests, where short-rotation, even-aged tree farming for loblolly pine is so prevalent. See Charles D. Canham, Nicole Rogers, and

Thomas Buchholz, "Regional Variation in Forest Harvest Regimes in the Northeastern United States," *Ecological Applications* 23 (2013): 515–22.

3. Each year the Environmental Protection Agency, under the United Nations Framework Convention on Climate Change, produces estimates of US greenhouse gas emissions and sinks. The "land use, land change and forestry" sector has typically been a bright spot in the report, since forest regrowth, particularly in the Northeast, has been a significant sink for carbon. For 2016 the report estimated that the nation's 302 million hectares of forest land sequestered the equivalent of 670 million metric tons of CO_2. That year 68 million metric tons were released to the atmosphere through conversion of forest land to development. https://www.epa.gov/sites/production/files/2018-01/documents/2018_chapter_6_land_use_land-use_change_and_forestry.pdf.

4. Thomas Buchholz, Charles D. Canham, and Stephen P. Hamburg, "Forest Biomass and Bioenergy: Opportunities and Constraints in the Northeastern United States," Cary Institute of Ecosystem Studies, Millbrook, NY (2011), https://www.caryinstitute.org/sites/default/files/public/downloads/news/report_biomass_2011.pdf.

5. John Daigle and colleagues report that twenty-three million acres of forestland changed ownership during the period from 1980 to 2005. Some of that land was likely bought and sold more than once. The total forestland in the four northern forest states is approximately forty-five million acres. See John J. Daigle, Lindsay Utley, Lisa C. Chase, Walter F. Kuentzel, and Tommy L. Brown, "Does New Large Private Landownership and Their Management Priorities Influence Public Access in the Northern Forest?" *Journal of Forestry* 110 (2012): 89–96.

6. My definition of "working forestland" is forestland, as defined by the Forest Inventory and Analysis program of the US Forest Service, on which logging is not legally prohibited (i.e., not reserved in their parlance). As I've mentioned elsewhere, the actual amount of truly available working forestland is much smaller because of landowner interests or a wide range of physical, biological, social, and economic factors that make logging extremely unlikely.

7. Colleagues and I have published three papers in recent years using forest inventory data to characterize regional forest harvest regimes. See Charles D. Canham, Nicole Rogers, and Thomas Buchholz, "Regional Variation in Forest Harvest Regimes in the Northeastern United States," *Ecological Applications* 23 (2013): 515–22; Jonathan R. Thompson, Charles D. Canham, Luca Morreale, David B. Kittredge, and Brett Butler, "Social and Biophysical Variation in Regional Timber Harvest Regimes," *Ecological Applications* 27

(2017): 942–55; and Michelle L. Brown, Charles D. Canham, Lora Murphy, and Therese M. Donovan, "Timber Harvest as the Predominant Disturbance Regime in Northeastern U.S. Forests: Effects of Harvest Intensification," *Ecosphere* 9 (2018): e02062. 10.1002/ecs2.2062. David Kittredge and colleagues analyzed forest harvest plans from the state of Massachusetts to characterize regional variation in forest management. See David B. Kittredge, Jonathan R. Thompson, Luca L. Morreale, Anne G. Short Gianotti, and Lucy R. Hutyra, "Three Decades of Forest Harvesting Along a Suburban–Rural Continuum," *Ecosphere* 8 (2017): e01882. 10.1002/ecs2.1882

8. Ecologists look at many attributes besides live tree biomass to define whether a forest can be truly considered old growth. Those attributes include the presence of very large individual trees, since their bark provides distinctive habitat for things like mosses and lichens. The presence of large amounts of standing and downed deadwood is also considered critical, since they too are unique environments for both plant and animal species.

9. See Brown et al., "Timber Harvest as the Predominant Disturbance Regime."

10. Total carbon sequestration will continue to grow even after total aboveground live biomass of trees stabilizes as carbon continues to accumulate in soils and in downed dead wood. These results come from the analyses by Brown et al., "Timber Harvest as the Predominant Disturbance Regime."

11. The issue of the net carbon emissions associated with forest-based bioenergy has been hotly debated. At this point, opposing sides appear to have decided to simply disagree and ignore each other. I have my own analysis of the pros and cons of each side of the debate and have outlined them in Charles D. Canham, "Carbon Cycle Implications of Forest Biomass Energy Production in the Northeastern United States," in Mike Jacobson and Daniel Ciolkosz, eds., *Wood-Based Energy in the Northern Forests,* 51–68 (New York: Springer, 2013).

12. The intense debates about whether forest biomass energy is carbon neutral ignore the fact that public policy related to biomass energy involves much more than simply its impact on greenhouse gas emissions. Much of the interest in forest bioenergy comes from the potential economic benefits to northern forest communities from the capital investment and jobs associated with biomass energy installations, at the scale from pellet stoves in individual homes to commercial-scale electricity generation.

13. In 2019, prices for offset credits on the California Air Resource Board carbon market were around thirteen dollars per ton of carbon dioxide equivalent. This would be roughly equivalent to twelve dollars per ton of wet wood. Landowners typically get only several dollars a ton for low-grade wood,

depending on their location and the species of wood. In areas lacking a strong market for low-grade wood, particularly in southern New England, it is not always easy for a landowner to even sell their low-grade wood.

14. The technology for selective logging has vastly improved in recent decades. It's now possible to do highly selective logging and remove the trees with little damage to trees left behind—either by going high tech with harvesters that can move carefully through a forest or low tech with draft horses.

15. See Philip M. Wargo, "Amino Nitrogen and Phenolic Constituents of Bark of American Beech, *Fagus grandifolia*, and Infestation by Beech Scale, *Cryptococcus fagisuga*," *European Journal of Forest Pathology* 18 (1988): 279–90; and Erika F. Latty, Charles. D. Canham, and Peter L. Marks, "Beech Bark Disease in Northern Hardwood Forests: The Importance of Nitrogen Dynamics and Forest History for Disease Incidence," *Canadian Journal of Forest Research—Revue canadienne de recherche forestière* 33 (2003): 257–68.

8

Change Is in the Air

1. Charles T. Driscoll, James N. Galloway, James F. Hornig, Gene E. Likens, Michael Oppenheimer, Kenneth A. Rahn, and David W. Schindler, "Is There Scientific Consensus on Acid Rain? Excerpts from Six Governmental Reports," Ad Hoc Committee on Acid Rain: Science and Policy, October 1985, Special Publication of the Institute of Ecosystem Studies, New York Botanical Garden, Millbrook, NY.

2. "Acid Rain Report Unleashes a Torrent of Criticism," by Philip Shabecoff, *New York Times,* March 20, 1990.

3. https://nsrcforest.org/project/surprising-growth-resurgence-red-spruce-northern-forest, Shelly A. Rayback, Department of Geography, University of Vermont.

4. R. Quinn Thomas, Charles D. Canham, Kathleen C. Weathers, and Christine L. Goodale, "Increased Tree Carbon Storage in Response to Nitrogen Deposition in the US," *Nature Geoscience* 3 (2010): 13–17.

5. Bin Wang, Herman H. Shugart, Jacquelyn K. Shuman, and Manual T. Lerdau, "Forests and Ozone: Productivity, Carbon Storage, and Feedbacks," *Scientific Reports* 6 (2016): 22133, doi:10.1038/srep22133

6. B. M. Bolker, S. W. Pacala, F. A. Bazzaz, C. D. Canham, and S. A. Levin, "Species Diversity and Ecosystem Response to Carbon Dioxide Fertilization: Conclusions from a Temperate Forest Model," *Global Change Biology* 1 (1995): 373–81.

7. The expansion of the US Forest Service forest inventory program to include monitoring of forest health was enacted in Public Law 100–521, The Forest Ecosystems and Atmospheric Pollution Research Act of 1988. The National Atmospheric Deposition Program (http://nadp.sws.uiuc.edu/) monitors several key components of air quality.

9
New and Unwelcome Passengers

1. Species nomenclature and taxonomic classifications change constantly, much to my annoyance since I have trouble remembering names. The Plant List, a global consortium that tries to referee the babel of competing plant names, has 160 accepted names for different species in the genus *Acer* worldwide. http://www.theplantlist.org/browse/A/Sapindaceae/Acer/.

2. Peter Marks, Robert Wesley, and Sana Gardescu have compiled a detailed study of these patterns for the Finger Lakes region of New York, in the context of changes in the flora of that region over the past two hundred years. Their analysis suggests that the number of native species has declined very slightly over that period due to local extirpation but not extinction of any species. The number of nonnative plant species has increased steadily throughout the two centuries, doubling from 19.5 percent of the flora in 1886 to 39 percent of the flora by 2005. See Peter L. Marks, F. Robert Wesley, and Sana Gardescu, "The Vascular Plant Diversity of the Finger Lakes Region of Central New York State: Changes in the 1800s and 1900s," *Journal of the Torrey Botanical Society* 135 (2008): 53–69. A comparable analysis of the proportions of native and introduced species in Britain can be found in M. J. Crawley, P. H. Harvey, and A. Purvis, "Comparative Ecology of the Native and Alien Floras of the British Isles," *Philosophical Transactions of the Royal Society London B* 351 (1996): 1251–59.

3. Károly Rédei, Zoltán Osváth-Bujtás, and Irina Veperdi, "Black Locust (*Robinia pseudoacacia* L.) Improvement in Hungary: A Review," *Acta Silvatica et Lignaria Hungarica* 4 (2008): 127–32.

4. Kurt Reinhart, Keith Clay, and colleagues have produced one of the best studied cases of the role of natural enemies in both the native distribution and invasion of a temperate tree species. Their study of the differences in the virulence of soil-borne pathogens in the native versus introduced range is presented in Kurt O. Reinhart, Tom Tytgat, Wim H. Van der Putten, and Keith Clay, "Virulence of Soil-Borne Pathogens and Invasion by *Prunus serotina*," *New Phytologist* 186 (2010): 484–95.

5. The analysis of the fraction of invasive species in the Finger Lakes region of New York that escaped from cultivation is presented in the 2008 paper by Peter Marks and colleagues, "Vascular Plant Diversity of the Finger Lakes Region." An analysis of introductions for woody plants nationally can be found in Sarah Hayden Reichard and Clement W. Hamilton, "Predicting Invasions of Woody Plants Introduced into North America," *Conservation Biology* 11 (1997): 193–203.

6. Patrick H. Martin, Charles D. Canham, and Peter L. Marks, "Why Forests Appear Resistant to Exotic Plant Invasions: Intentional Introductions, Stand Dynamics, and the Role of Shade Tolerance," *Frontiers in Ecology and the Environment* 7 (2009): 142–49.

7. See Kristina A. Stinson, Stuart A. Campbell, Jeff R. Powell, Benjamin E. Wolfe, Ragan M. Callaway, Giles C. Thelen, Steven G. Hallett, Daniel Prati, and John N. Klironomos, "Invasive Plant Suppresses the Growth of Native Tree Seedlings by Disrupting Belowground Mutualisms," *Public Library of Science Biology* 4(5): e140 [doi:10.1371/journal.pbio.0040140]; and Ragan M. Callaway, Don Cipollini, Kathryn Barto, Giles C. Thelen, Steven G. Hallett, Daniel Prati, Kristina Stinson, and John Klironomos, "Novel Weapons: Invasive Plant Suppresses Fungal Mutualists in America but Not in Its Native Europe," *Ecology* 89 (2008): 1043–55.

8. Patrick Martin took the lead on our studies of Norway maple, while Lorena Gómez-Aparicio focused on tree of heaven. Between them they covered all of the life history stages needed to incorporate these two species in SORTIE-ND, our model of forest dynamics. Gómez-Aparicio's work included a novel approach to the characterization of allelopathy under realistic field conditions, a subject previously limited to greenhouse and laboratory assays with uncertain applicability in the field. Examples of their work include Lorena Gómez-Aparicio and Charles D. Canham, "Neighbourhood Analyses of the Allelopathic Effects of the Invasive Tree *Ailanthus altissima* in Temperate Forests," *Journal of Ecology* 96 (2008): 447–58; and Patrick H. Martin and Charles D. Canham, "Dispersal and Recruitment Limitation in Native Versus Exotic Tree Species: Life-History Strategies and Janzen-Connell Effects," *Oikos* 119 (2010): 807–24.

9. This paper by Patrick Bohlen and colleagues is a good, if now somewhat dated, summary of the ecology of earthworm invasion. Patrick J. Bohlen, Stefan Scheu, Cindy M. Hale, Mary Ann McLean, Sonja Migge, Peter M. Groffman, and Dennis Parkinson, "Non-Native Invasive Earthworms as Agents of Change in Northern Temperate Forests," *Frontiers in Ecology and the Environment* 2 (2004): 427–35. For an example of the kinds of methods used to study the effects of earthworm invasion, see Cindy M. Hale, Lee E.

Frelich, Peter B. Reich, and John Pastor, "Exotic Earthworm Effects on Hardwood Forest Floor, Nutrient Availability and Native Plants: A Mesocosm
Study," *Oecologia* 155 (2008): 509–18.

10. Everyone who works on invasive species must have a few that provoke
the most intense nightmares. For me, that species is the Japanese knotweed
(*Polygonum cuspidatum*), followed closely by the common reed, *Phragmites
australis*. While knotweed can be found in forests, it is much more aggressive
in open environments, particularly along rivers and streams, where it can
take over a gravel bar in the summer with an impenetrable thicket two meters
tall. Aside from ruining a canoer's ability to pull out for a picnic on a gravel
bar while paddling down a wild river, knotweed threatens one of the most
unique plant communities in the Adirondacks: herbaceous species found
along gravel bars in what are known as ice meadows. The native species are
not shade tolerant, and rafts of ice each winter and spring keep woody plants
from taking over. But Japanese knotweed is a perennial and can establish and
regrow from its roots each year, effectively eliminating the unique habitat
offered by the ice meadows. Both state agencies and regional conservation
groups recognize the problem, but some of the most effective efforts to control knotweed in the Adirondacks have been led by a group of local volunteers,
organized by Douglas Johnson, a physician from Massachusetts who has a
summer home in the region. He and all of the volunteers have my gratitude.

11. I can't think of another environmental issue that has motivated as
much volunteer effort as the battle against invasive species. So much so that
both state agencies and regional conservation groups have worked very effectively to engage the public on this issue. In New York State that engagement
has taken the form of what are known as Partnerships for Regional Invasive
Species Management, or PRISMs. The eight PRISMs around the state are
modeled on a program first developed by the Nature Conservancy's Adirondack Chapter.

12. This would not be true if you were trying to identify mosses and lichens,
which are not vascular plants, as you went along; partly that is because identifying the mosses often requires a microscope.

10

A Far More Threatening Invasion

1. Andrew (Sandy) Liebhold and colleagues published a map of the
numbers of damaging invasive forest pests per county for the United States in
2013. The greatest number (close to forty-five) occur in the Northeast, centered

around New York City. One of the most surprising patterns is the relatively low number of pests along the Gulf Coast, even though some of the busiest ports in the country are located there. See Andrew M. Liebhold, Deborah G. McCullough, Laura M. Blackburn, Susan J. Frankel, Betsy Von Holle, and Juliann E. Aukema, "A Highly Aggregated Geographical Distribution of Forest Pest Invasions in the USA," *Diversity and Distributions* 19 (2013): 1208–16.

2. Andrew M. Liebhold, Eckehard G. Brockerhoff, Lynn J. Garrett, Jennifer L. Parke, and Kerry O. Britton, "Live Plant Imports: The Major Pathway for Forest Insect and Pathogen Invasions of the US," *Frontiers in Ecology and the Environment* 10 (2012): 135–43.

3. Ibid

4. Brian Leung, Michael R. Springborn, James A. Turner, and Eckehard G. Brockerhoff, "Pathway-Level Risk Analysis: The Net Present Value of an Invasive Species Policy in the US," *Frontiers in Ecology and the Environment* 12 (2014): 273–79.

5. Christian Marks provides a wonderful summary of the ecological role of American elm in floodplain forests of the Northeast. See https://www.fs.fed .us/nrs/pubs/gtr/gtr-nrs-p-174papers/10marks-gtr-p-174.pdf. The three elm species in the eastern US, American elm, slippery elm, and winged elm (*Ulmus alata*, a Gulf Coast species), still rank among the fifty most common tree species in the region despite decimation by Dutch elm disease. Our models predict continued slow, gradual decline in abundance of both northeastern elm species. But not enough is known for us to have any confidence in their long-term fate.

6. Aaron M. Ellison, Michael S. Bank, Barton D. Clinton, Elizabeth A. Colburn, Katherine Elliott, Chelcy R. Ford, David R. Foster, Brian D. Kloeppel, Jennifer D. Knoepp, Gary M. Lovett, Jacqueline Mohan, David A. Orwig, Nicholas L. Rodenhouse, William V. Sobczak, Kristina A. Stinson, Jeffrey K. Stone, Christopher M. Swan, Jill Thompson, Betsy Von Holle, and Jackson R. Webster, "Loss of Foundation Species: Consequences for the Structure and Dynamics of Forested Ecosystems," *Frontiers in Ecology and the Environment* 3 (2005): 479–86.

7. Melissa Youngquist and coauthors provide a summary of likely changes due to loss of black ash from wetlands. See Melissa B. Youngquist, Sue L. Eggert, Anthony W. D'Amato, Brian J. Palik, and Robert A. Slesak, "Potential Effects of Foundation Species Loss on Wetland Communities: A Case Study of Black Ash Wetlands Threatened by Emerald Ash Borer," *Wetlands* 37 (2017): 787–99.

8. See R. Talbot Trotter III and Kathleen S. Shields, "Variation in Winter Survival of the Invasive Hemlock Woolly Adelgid (Hemiptera: Adelgidae)

Across the Eastern United States," *Environmental Entomology* 38 (2009): 577–87; and Elizabeth Butin, Adam H. Porter, and Joseph Elkinton, "Adaptation During Biological Invasions and the Case of *Adelges tsugae*," *Evolutionary Ecology Research* 7 (2005): 887–900.

9. We did not observe much outright mortality of trees other than understory hemlocks immediately following the gypsy moth outbreak of 1980–81. But a resampling in 2006 of permanent plots established in 1984 in the Cary Institute woods showed significant mortality of chestnut oaks, which could well be due to lingering effects of the previous defoliation (as well as more minor defoliation in 1989 and 1990). See Daniel S. Katz, Gary M. Lovett, Charles D. Canham, and Catherine M. O'Reilly, "Legacies of Land Use History Diminish over 22 Years in a Forest in Southeastern New York," *Journal of the Torrey Botanical Society* 137 (2010): 236–51.

10. Juliann E. Aukema, Brian Leung, Kent Kovacs, Corey Chivers, Kerry O. Britton, Jeffrey Englin, Susan J. Frankel, Robert G. Haight, Thomas P. Holmes, Andrew M. Liebhold, Deborah G. McCullough, and Betsy Von Holle, "Economic Impacts of Non-Native Forest Insects in the Continental United States," *PLoS ONE* 6 (2011): e24587, doi:10.1371/journal.pone.0024587.

11. Gary M. Lovett, Marissa Weiss, Andrew M. Liebhold, Thomas P. Holmes, Brian Leung, Kathy Fallon Lambert, David A. Orwig, Faith T. Campbell, Jonathan Rosenthal, Deborah G. McCullough, Radka Wildova, Matthew P. Ayres, Charles D. Canham, David R. Foster, Shannon L. LaDeau, and Troy Weldy, "Nonnative Forest Insects and Pathogens in the United States: Impacts and Policy Options," *Ecological Applications* 26 (2016): 1437–55. The specific proposals that constitute Tree-SMART Trade are described online at https://www.caryinstitute.org/science-program/research-projects/tree-smart-trade.

12. By way of disclaimer, I was a coauthor on the 2016 paper by Lovett and colleagues but had no role in the development of the Tree-SMART Trade proposals. But my longtime colleague Gary Lovett has my undying gratitude for taking on this challenge.

13. Alexander M. Evans, "The Speed of Invasion: Rates of Spread for Thirteen Exotic Forest Insects and Diseases," *Forests* 7 (2016), doi:10.3390/f7050099.

14. Some plant species have seeds that can remain dormant for decades while buried in the soil. But only one of the common northeastern tree species, pin cherry (*Prunus pennsylvanica*), has this trait. So buried seeds are not a viable repository in nature for most northeastern tree species. But seeds of most of our tree species can be kept indoors in archives under controlled conditions.

11

Storm Clouds Looming

1. Lora Murphy and I present our analyses of the climate sensitivities of the demography of the fifty most common tree species in the eastern United States in three papers: (1) Charles D. Canham and Lora Murphy, "The Demography of Tree Species Response to Climate: Seedling Recruitment and Survival," *Ecosphere* 7 (2016): e01424. 10.1002/ecs2.1424; (2) Charles D. Canham and Lora Murphy, "The Demography of Tree Species Response to Climate: Sapling and Canopy Tree Growth," *Ecosphere* 7 (2016): e01474. 10.1002/ecs2.1474; and (3) Charles D. Canham and Lora Murphy, "The Demography of Tree Species Response to Climate: Sapling and Canopy Tree Survival," *Ecosphere* 8 (2017): e01701. 10.1002/ecs2.1701.

2. Details of this analysis are in Charles D. Canham, and R. Quinn Thomas, "Frequency, Not Relative Abundance, of Temperate Tree Species Varies Along Climate Gradients in Eastern North America," *Ecology* 91 (2010): 3433–40. The only consistent evidence of variation in relative abundance of tree species as a function of climate was that some species have slightly higher relative abundance at the northern edges of their ranges. This could simply be due to the fact that there are fewer species to share the canopy with as you move northward because of the well-known latitudinal decline in tree species diversity. Patrick Martin of Denver University and I recently completed a similar analysis for the distributions of species in the interior West (Rocky Mountain) region of the United States and found broadly similar results.

3. Kerry D. Woods and Margaret B. Davis, "Paleoecology of Range Limits: Beech in the Upper Peninsula of Michigan," *Ecology* 70 (1989): 681–96.

4. Examples of very different models that come to similar conclusions about the slow pace of eastern forest response to climate change include Wen J. Wang, Hong S. He, Frank R. Thompson III, Jacob S. Fraser, Brice B. Hanberry, and William D. Dijak, "Changes in Forest Biomass and Tree Species Distribution under Climate Change in the Northeastern United States," *Landscape Ecology* 32 (2017): 1399–1413; and Jonathan R. Thompson, David R. Foster, Robert Scheller, and David Kittredge, "The Influence of Land Use and Climate Change on Forest Biomass and Composition in Massachusetts, USA," *Ecological Applications* 21 (2011): 2425–44.

5. The notion that tree species migration will proceed via establishment of small satellite outliers beyond a slowly advancing wave front, with gradual backfilling behind the satellite populations, is also an apt description of the

way most introduced forest pests and pathogens have spread across the northeastern United States.

6. Examples of recent studies of frost damage following early spring leaf-out include Carol K. Augspurger, "Reconstructing Patterns of Temperature, Phenology, and Frost Damage over 124 Years: Spring Damage Risk Is Increasing," *Ecology* 94 (2013): 41–50; and Koen Hufkens, Mark A. Friedl, Trevor F. Keenan, Oliver Sonnentag, Amey Bailey, John O'Keefe, and Andrew D. Richardson, "Ecological Impacts of a Widespread Frost Event Following Early Spring Leaf-Out," *Global Change Biology* 18 (2012): 2365–77.

7. Barbara Bentz and colleagues review the potential effects of climate change on bark beetles in Barbara J. Bentz, Jacques Régnière, Christopher J. Fettig, E. Matthew Hansen, Jane L. Hayes, Jeffrey A. Hicke, Rick G. Kelsey, Jose F. Negrón, and Steven J. Seybold, "Climate Change and Bark Beetles of the Western United States and Canada: Direct and Indirect Effects," *BioScience* 60 (2010): 602–13. The link between needle blight outbreaks and wetter summers in British Columbia is reported in Alex Woods, K. David Coates, and Andreas Hamann, "Is an Unprecedented Dothistroma Needle Blight Epidemic Related to Climate Change?" *BioScience* 55 (2005): 761–69.

8. The results of our study of local differentiation in tree ring response to variation in climate are reported in Charles D. Canham, Lora Murphy, Rachel Riemann, Richard McCullough, and Elizabeth Burrill, "Local Differentiation in Tree Growth Responses to Climate," *Ecosphere* 9 (2018): e02368. 10.1002/ecs2.2368.

12

What Lies Ahead?

1. May Theilgaard Watts's classic "Reading the Landscape of America" (Nature Study Guild Publishers) was published in 1957, with a second edition in 1975. "Reading the Forested Landscape: A Natural History of New England" (Countryman Press) by Tom Wessells and coauthors covers the same topic with a tighter focus on northeastern forests.

2. Roughly every decade for the past fifty years the US Forest Service has been required to issue projections of the likely trends in forest inventory data over the coming decades, including projected forest growth and harvests and the surplus in growth over mortality and harvests (i.e., the net change in forest biomass). Thomas Buchholz and coauthors reviewed those projections and found that projections of even just ten years into the future were never more accurate than simply assuming no change. My assessment is that the

major source of discrepancy between the projections and reality was not in the underlying biology of tree growth and forest productivity but in the inability to forecast economic trends that determined forest harvest rates. See Thomas Buchholz, Stephen Prisley, Gregg Marland, Charles Canham, and Neil Sampson, "Uncertainty in Projecting GHG Emissions from Bioenergy," *Nature Climate Change* 4 (2014): 1045–47.

Index